Educational Values for

School Leadership

The Management and Leadership in Education Series

Series Editor: Howard Green

Competences for School Managers Derek Esp
Educational Values for School Leadership Sylvia West

Educational Values for School Leadership

Sylvia West

KOGAN PAGE

London • Philadelphia

First published in 1993

Kogan Page Limited
120 Pentonville Road
London N1 9JN

© Sylvia West, 1993

British Library Cataloguing in Publication Data

A CIP record of this book is available from the British Library.

ISBN 0 7494 0839 1

Typeset by Saxon Graphics Ltd, Derby
Printed and bound in Great Britain by Biddles Ltd, Guildford and King's Lynn.

Contents

Series Editor's Foreword

The Government's educational reforms have created an unprecedented rate of change in schools. They have also raised many fundamental questions about the purpose of education and the nature of school management and leadership. Similar changes are occurring in many other educational systems throughout the world. There is an urgent need for all of us with an interest in education to step back and reflect on recent educational reforms, to reaffirm old truths and successful practice where necessary, to sift out the best of the changes, modifying or abandoning those which are a distraction from the central purpose of schools: to ensure that an education of high quality is a guaranteed opportunity for *all* our children and young people.

This series has been carefully conceived to satisfy the growing need for short, readable books, designed for busy people and with a focus on issues at the cutting edge of school management and leadership.

These books are written by reflective practitioners rather than theorists. The authors include heads, advisers, inspectors, education officers, trainers and governors who are working at the sharp end, trying to make sense of the welter of change and with a common desire to contribute to a strong and continually improving system of education in the UK. The series celebrates the ideals, skills and expertise of professionals in education who want to work in partnership with all the other stakeholders in our schools.

In this book, Sylvia West provides a penetrating and thoughtful analysis of the central question: what are schools for? For those who have leadership and management responsibilities, finding an answer to this question must start with a focus on values.

Drawing on her own experience as a head and on a research project which involved extended interviews with other heads and chairs of governors from a variety of schools, Sylvia West challenges schools to involve all the main stakeholders – staff, pupils, parents and governors – in seeking to identify the values which should inform and inspire their work.

The challenge will not be comfortable for many but it must be faced. The response will not be the same from all schools and it is right that it should not be: good schools can emerge from a variety of leadership styles and management practices. However, the important common ground is that each school has been through the process of clarifying values and implementing them, involving all its main partners. Having done this, we may possibly bring together the ideals of choice, diversity and achievement for all pupils, with the school as an integrative and socially cohesive influence in the local community.

Howard Green
Eggbuckland
October 1992

Preface and Acknowledgements

This book has been written during perhaps the busiest period of my life: my school, like many others, is caught up in the pressures of change and new legislation. My determination that it should nevertheless be written despite such pressures reflects a conviction that present circumstances, more than ever, demand shared comment and values. The pace of change and the rushed consultation which surrounds much of its enactment require reflection as well as action; it is the latter, often precipitate, which so often takes precedence. I attempt here to reflect on educational values in a world of accelerating operational change. Though a week is a long time in education, to adapt the famous comment on politics, I trust that the underlying message of the book, while reflecting current events, transcends them to point to directions and values which are fundamental and forward-looking.

First, I would like to thank Howard Green, in his capacity of Director of the National Educational Assessment Centre, Oxfordshire, for his support while I carried out the Values Project for NEAC, and as Editor of the series; also the heads and governors who gave the project the gift of precious time; and the Gulbenkian Foundation who made it possible.

Second, I would like to thank Dr John Schostak, University of East Anglia, for his stimulating conversations and support of my research and writing. I would like to thank also my Chair of Governors for his support, my Cambridgeshire colleagues, and in particular the Director of Education, John Ferguson, for their general support, and my

9

secretary for explaining the mysteries of the word-processor to a now converted Luddite.

Finally, I would like to thank my husband for the endless cups of tea, encouragement and patience!

Abbreviations

CEA	Community Education Association
CLEA	Council of Local Education Authorities
CSCS	Centre for the Study of the Comprehensive School
CTC	City Technology College
GMS	Grant-Maintained Status
INSET	In-Service Training
LEA	Local Education Authority
LMS	Local Management of Schools
NAVET	National Association for Values in Education and Training
NEAC	National Educational Assessment Centre (a training and development centre for heads, deputies and governors)
PRISE	Programme for Reform in Secondary Education
PSVME	Personal, Social, Vocational and Moral Education (The Personal and Social Development Programme at Impington Village College)
RSA	Royal Society of Arts
TANEA	Towards a New Education Act

Introduction:

Managing the Values of Schools

Political, professional and popular values

> Education policy and values interact with the moods and circumstances of their periods. Education is a social artefact embodying aspirations about the good life for the individual and the best arrangements for the whole society. It is, therefore, particularly prone to change as social and economic circumstances change (Kogan, 1985, p 11).

The effect of Government reforms in education is to put schools squarely into the market place, where heads and governors find themselves managing not only the resources and curriculum but increasingly also the disparate values of a customer-driven culture. Greater political direction of education threatens to deprofessionalize teachers in terms of their pedagogical expertise as teaching methods and syllabuses are increasingly circumscribed: its more competitive systems also threaten professional corporate purposes and relationships. Local authority infrastructures, which in many instances have promoted collegial and community values, are being dismantled as schools are being encouraged to operate as independent entities, caught between a more centralized political direction and popular control.

Despite their position between these poles, and indeed precisely because of it, heads and governors of schools are inevitably pivotal mediators and managers of values. The role of school leaders is increasingly defined by a need to mediate between often conflicting values: professional values, political values and customer values.

New skills and strategies

Faced with the problematic nature of such a position, school leaders need to review the competencies and strategies which will prevent the best of critical and creative thinking in educational professionalism succumbing to:

(1) a purely reactive and technician role which delivers an educational product rather like a factory worker might manage a production line

(2) a fragmentation of corporate and community purposes.

It is the purpose of this book to suggest that critical professional thinking and corporate values will only be fostered and refined through more attention by school leaders to the promotion of educated and active communities. Schools must bring value questions associated with education to the fore in their communities, despite the fact that in the market place the temptation for heads and governors, reliant on numbers of children for resourcing, is to dazzle and seduce potential customers with manipulative images and value packages tailored to perceived public taste.

Though many school leaders would welcome any trend away from the rather paternalistic professionalism which has existed in the past, and possibly still does exist in some institutions, there is the danger that the ferocity of competition and fragmentation of education in the present climate might drive even the most open and enlightened of school managers into something of a siege mentality. It may be difficult for professionals to see the 'deep' involvement and scrutiny of parents and the community, recommended in the White Paper (DfE, 1992), as other than threat and interference against a backdrop of political interventionism. However, the involvement of parents and communities has already been the mission of many 'community schools'. In such a definition I would not only include colleges like my own which are shaped in the Henry Morris tradition of designated centres for education 'cradle to the grave', but any school which has ensured an outreaching and participative climate in their community at large.

The concept of community colleges as envisaged and founded by Henry Morris, the enlightened Secretary of Education in Cambridgeshire in the 1920s and 1930s, is no less relevant today and indeed his vision, though resting on the somewhat more paternalistic conventions of his period, still provides inspiration in the mood and circumstances of today. In his village colleges Morris sought to compensate for rural deprivation. Today's deprivation is perhaps of a different order: it is a deprivation of mechanisms to express common values and purposes. Thus today's community mission for schools has the same ultimate purpose as Morris envisaged for them despite new 'moods and circumstances', as his own words testify:

> The whole welfare of communities and the vigour and prosperity of their intellectual and social life depends on the extent to which centres of unfettered initiative can be developed within them. In the state, frankly organizing itself as an educational institution, freedom and richness will be secured by the development within the state of large numbers of adult autonomous societies. They will be the guarantees for intellectual and spiritual freedom, the surest bulwark against the tyranny of the state in politics, industry, religion, science and art (Morris, 1926/1984, p 41).

Schools as integrative forces

In the following chapters the importance for effective and visionary management of applying clearly articulated values to open and participative processes in the school is explored and affirmed. In the disintegrative culture of our times, the bombshell of educational change would seem to be reinforcing the silence which surrounds our quest for common values. Schools are not just centres for the education of children, they are also centres for the hopes and aspirations of whole communities, often divided against themselves or simply cut off from each other by anonymizing processes such as lack of roots, extended family, or common work or play. Schools cannot help to restore communities entirely but they can in their management of community values, in as far as they heed and meet them, encourage either mutual education or compound silences. In the model which school managers choose for managing their schools, they can either work towards new forms of openness and participation where values are concerned, or manipulate the loss of corporateness and common vision which already exists and is exemplified in a customer ethic.

To suggest a responsibility to school management beyond the pressures already being experienced may seem foolish indeed – a call for super-management perhaps. However, if schools do not manage to find ways in the new fragmentation to combat as far as possible a trend of disintegration where values are concerned, their cultural mission will fall between the stools of political and popular control to the detriment of all.

Who educates the super-managers?

That there was, and is, a lack of confidence among heads and deputies in dealing with values issues was confirmed to Howard Green, the then Director of the National Educational Assessment Centre, Oxfordshire, one of the training centres which through joint funding of industry and the Department for Education is offering development programmes for heads, when he met a number of Her Majesty's Inspectors in summer 1991. After considering a large number of school development plans during various inspections across the country, it was clear that the rhetoric of these plans did not always match practice. Inspectors found that the schools which had most effectively implemented their plans were those where values were clearly articulated by the head as a fundamental basis of school planning. In such schools, too, the stakeholders – staff, governors, parents and pupils – would be seen to have their contribution to make in realizing the school's vision and plans.

NEAC decided that there was enough indication of a direct link between effective practice and leadership in the field of values to warrant further research into the management of values, which would inform a head's development programme and provide urgently needed leadership skills for heads, and indeed governors, in their more accountable positions.

With, therefore, the generous sponsorship of the Gulbenkian Foundation, which has a particular interest in the development of school ethos, a research project was commissioned by NEAC to investigate the link between values management and effective school leadership. In the NEAC survey fourteen heads and nine chairs of governors and one vice-chair were interviewed between September and December 1991, and their educational philosophy and values explored in some depth, together with their reflection on the impact of external cultural and political change. Although this was a relatively small sample, the interviewees represented a wide range of likely value bases of different educational sectors, namely state, grant-maintained, city technology college and the independent sector. They represented, too, different age-phasing in the secondary sector and different socio-economic backgrounds. Seven local authorities were included with a spread of rural, commuter areas, city, and deprived urban contexts.

Managing values in context

The project recognized that heads and schools do not operate within a vacuum in relation to values. The external context impacts upon the values of institutions and predetermines to some extent their room for manoeuvre; but there is also in any educational endeavour a continual striving for something superior which takes the human race forward in its attempts at perfectibility in spite of all constraint, as Kogan describes (my italics):

> Values are moral propensities or feelings about *what ought to be*. They underpin ideologies which are value preferences attached to some kind of programme for, or aspiration to, action. Changes in values must be set in their *context* of movements in social arrangements and assumptions, and in the state of the economy. Values themselves become a context in which other factors affecting policies are grounded. Values are implicit in the power and institutional relations which are both the contexts and the results of different value positions (Kogan, 1985, p 11).

Thus, as schools find themselves caught between political and popular control, there is a need for a new professionalism to assert itself in our schools. It will not be one that flies in the face of a popular mood away from paternalism and forms which anonymize the individual. It will rather retain the strength of our educational traditions in terms of providing a critical voice which queries the pitfalls of political prescription and popular values by encouraging a greater examination of those values, not on *behalf* of communities but *with* communities. To encourage such examination schools must be prepared to open their values to themselves and their communities: staff, governors, parents, pupils, and the wider community. An emphasis on value questions rather than value packaging is not easy to effect in a market ethic but its importance lies in encouraging speaking up and participation.

The head seeking to articulate and implement his or her vision has to start from a clear awareness of the school's context – both in terms of its community and its boundaries as defined by political decisions. Thus, Chapter 1 deals with the context of schools and the management possibilities within that context. Then, calling on my own experience in headship over 12 years in different schools and the living experiences of the voices emerging from the Gulbenkian/NEAC survey, positive mechanisms are explored to establish Morris's 'centres of unfettered initiative' within 'autonomous societies' for individuals who are persons rather than customers and members of a community rather than isolates. 'Community schools' are not a political or foolproof solution to the potential fragmentation of a market ideology but they are an important cog in the empowerment skills and process needed for *reconstruction* in an increasingly *deconstructed* culture.

Chapter 1
School Values in Context

Diversity or fragments?

The market system which allows for parental choice of schools rests very much on what Albert O. Hirschman, in *Exit, Voice and Loyalty* (1970), terms the discipline of 'exit'. If parents do not like what is on offer they can ostensibly vote with their feet. The alternative is the 'voice' option which engages with the organization to express dissatisfaction about the service or product in the hope of redress. The more diverse the market the less will customers rely on voice and the more on exit, which denies the unfavoured institution any negotiation or relationship with that customer, but brings the customer a more immediate satisfaction of his or her wishes. It is just this diversity which the White Paper (1992) envisages and which John Butcher MP, in an address to the Royal Society of Arts in 1990, saw as analogous to the freedoms emerging at the time in Eastern Europe:

> Where, therefore, am I moving in terms of an organizational and practical approach to the training and education needs of the nineties ... I have argued for more pluralism, dissemination of power and responsibilities and pushing cash upstream, cutting out middlemen, cutting out people who get in the way or people who just want to share out the misery equally between competing institutions ... I am on the side of the Muscovite housewife. In terms of his top-down methodology I am not on the side of Mr Gorbachev.

John Butcher saw no further need in such freedom for there to be political nominees on governing bodies and he saw, too, local authorities withering on the vine. Heads would be released, he stated jubilantly, from the 'general political background ... They should be released from it, if we are going to have this new more responsive, more free regime.'

Clearly in such thinking, which is echoed very closely in the White Paper (1992), there is little place for the macro view of society or of educational philosophy and planning. What John Butcher, and subsequently John Patten in his White Paper, term diversity, others might term fragmentation of the state system: thousands of schools are envisaged opting out of local authority control and thus local planning; this aside from the City Technology Colleges (CTCs) which have been set up in urban areas. Yet the White Paper implicitly rejects such doubt in its assumption throughout of commonsense principles; this stance is typified in the Foreword to it written by the Prime Minister, John Major:

> Our reforms rest on commonsense principles – more parental choice; rigorous testing and external inspection of standards in schools; transfer of responsibility to individual schools and their governors; and, above all, an insistence that every pupil everywhere has the same opportunities through a good common grounding in key subjects. Few people would now argue with these principles. They are all helping to shape a more open, a more responsive and a more demanding system of education.

Nevertheless, there are those who do argue with such 'commonsense', not least the former Chief Inspector of Schools, Eric Bolton, who in an address to local authorities (1992, paras 19, 21, 23), expressed his grave reservations about the reforms:

> it is surely a triumph of hope over experience to expect that such self-interested, isolated, fragmented decisions, made in thousands of separate institutions, will add up to a sensible, effective and efficient national system ... It cannot, however, remain a public and equitable national service, compulsory for some part of its time, if it is to be shaped and determined by nothing other than the aggregation of the random, self-interested choices made by individuals in thousands of particular schools. A public education service must be subject to some degree of overall planning and organization ... [it] not only requires some national and local organization

planning if it is to be effective and equitable, it needs a vision; an underpinning philosophy.

Words and meanings

However, there is a consistency attached to the Government's reforms, as comparison of John Butcher's view (1990) with the stance of the 1992 White Paper indicates. The White Paper reasserts John Butcher's 'vision' and represents a consolidation of a Conservative agenda which persisted throughout the 1980s and continues to be pursued into the 1990s. However, how far such an agenda does reflect common assent cannot be measured for *common sense* is in fact the rub. Words attach to values and ways of seeing the world; they mean different things to different people and they change their meanings as circumstances and perceptions change. Modern linguistical sciences document this very clearly. If one is to discover the difference behind words, there has to be some attempt to 'unpack' meanings. In the cut and thrust of public rhetoric it is difficult to find space and time to do this and thus words which are attached to powerful mechanisms of change become powerful words and ultimately powerful ideas.

The remarkable feature of the White Paper is its emphasis on *organizational diversity* which does not admit of a *diversity of sense or meaning* in society at large; it does not admit either of any need to examine the cultural aims which should underpin its changes, as John White (1990, p 13), writing on the 1988 National Curriculum statements, emphasizes:

> It's amazing how wrong one can be. It is nearly 20 years since I first began to argue for a national curriculum. In all that time, I have been assuming ... a pretty complex task. [One] would have to work at a coherent and defensible set of overall aims ... [however] the British Government ... showed that devising a national curriculum is simplicity itself. You pick ten foundation subjects to fill most of the school timetable, highlight three as of particular importance and arrange for tests at different stages. I could have worked out the national curriculum years ago. Anyone could.

What John White saw as a simplistic approach is not such a surprising outcome in our society. Education has always evolved from the values and 'beliefs entertained by individuals or groups of individuals [which] become policies when power is gained and the values become

21

authoritative. Some policy movements derive less from a priori assumptions about what is morally right than from the observation and experience of practitioners' (Kogan, 1985, p 18).

'Vision' has only ever been in the hands of individuals who have influenced education gradually and in diffuse manner. It has been the very absence of any absolute 'vision' or any monopoly of thinking which has allowed this influence to operate and grow, though equally, of course, it has also allowed great ideas to fade or die. The fact is that there is no public tradition in this country of regarding education as the cultural linchpin of social aims and meanings because there is no tradition in our society of establishing the fundamental aims and principles of our social institutions, as R.H.Tawney explains (1921, p 1):

> It is a commonplace that the characteristic virtue of Englishmen is their power of sustained practical activity, and their characteristic vice a reluctance to test the quality of that activity by reference to principles. They are incurious as to theory, take fundamentals for granted, and are more interested in the state of the roads than their place on the map.

A muddle of inherited assumptions

This tendency to muddle through on inherited assumptions and unquestioned conventions has been both a strength of British society as well as a weakness. As John White (1987, p 14) recognizes, the Government's 'initiatives have followed through the logic of the shift from professional to political control as far as seeing that a coherent education system requires a coherent value-underpinning', however, there has been no process to date in our modern and pluralistic society for there to be any public and coherent working out of these values. Instead, the value-product of education continues to be assumed beneath a focus on increasingly speedy operational change.

The Great Debate, instigated by James Callaghan in his Ruskin College speech, 16 October 1976, began something of a discussion but the grandiose claim to a Great Debate is rather wide of the mark. Beyond an emphasis on education's relevance to industry and some recognition of the need for a more 'hands-on' approach, there has been no rigorous examination of the cultural values which might inform the society for which education is preparing future citizens. Such complex questions have been placed by political decisions into:

(1) the hands of an abstract mechanism, namely the regulatory, or rather deregulatory, force of the market, and,
(2) the hands of the Secretary of State for Education who now holds considerable central powers over all aspects of school organization and curriculum.

It is a policy for education which demonstrates a curious blend of laissez-faire principles and strong centralized control which, if it continues, leaves our educational future resting between two poles, namely consumer public and central political control.

The questions and criticisms raised by Callaghan's Ruskin speech instigated an impetus for change but this seems to have preceded a full appraisal of what needed to be changed and why. We have now in the reforms a concern to discipline the system and to make it more *effective and efficient* without any fundamental questioning of its *essential values and aims*, because the Government assumes, perhaps capturing an anxious public mood anguished by modern uncertainties, that the public wants a recognizable, largely traditional value-product. This assumption has closed down debate, and operational decisions to effect this product have taken over. However, operational change cannot be divorced from value-emphasis; in other words the medium is the message.

A culture in crisis?

Indeed, the responses of Government to the reform of education reflect the difficulties which face today's society as a whole. Moral values, often assumed in our culture rather than explored, are becoming in the scientific scepticism of our age increasingly privatized and invisible. One would imagine with John White (1990, p 16) that 'the aims and content of education are intimately connected with views about the kind of society we wish to live in'. However, this is precisely the problem. How do we, in the modern circumstances of a multi-faith and faithless society and in the absence of any national constitution such as the American Bill of Rights, achieve social, philosophical, cultural, spiritual and political consensus on what education should be aiming to do?

It is not surprising in such circumstances that the Government has skirted around any real debate in education. It has preferred to assemble the traditional subjects, has added Technology, an element of Christian morality and heritage in the form of the Act of Collective Worship and tighter controls of religious syllabuses, but has otherwise left any resolving of political, social and cultural aims to take care of themselves. Any value-conflicts which might arise from the absence of legitimated macro aims are left to the schools and their stakeholders to work out.

Of course, the National Curriculum and the White Paper do carry values and aims, even if they are not perceived to be that coherent or particularly profound. However, the absence of any publicly examined macro-coherence to the reforms mirrors a culture in crisis and transition; we are not at all sure as a society where we are going – a state of affairs characteristic of nearly every age but exacerbated in this century by the fact of rapid change. Henry Morris, the 'visionary' Secretary for Education in Cambridgeshire and founder of the concept of the community college, articulated a similar sense of crisis as long ago as 1926 (Morris, 1926/1984, pp 36-7), and, despite great strides forward in education, including community education, there is still no room for complacency today:

> The effects of the disintegration and secularization of life are to be seen on every hand, especially in the profound spiritual futility of our state system of education ... The state system has ... arisen in a period of intellectual and political confusion. It has been divorced and is divorced from a great imaginative conception of the significance and destiny of human life, and it has not been nourished by a great political conception of the community ... It is the life that the adult will lead, the working philosophy by which he will live, the politics of the community which he will serve in his maturity, that should be the main concern of education. Unless education is concerned with these, frames the values, influences them and adumbrates them, then the education of the young will be in vain.

However, the exploration of such values sits ill with a society whose technology and pace require quick decisions and certainties rather than what Tawney's practical Englishman might see as Hamlet-like delay and introspection. The focus generally today is on activism, operationalism and instrumentalism, for they appear amid our value uncertainty as easier to measure and manage. The disintegration and secularization of which Morris speaks has gathered further pace since 1926 and though traditional authority and morality have been increasingly questioned in this century, we have not yet formulated a new order. We are living on what Nietzsche (1965, p 11) termed 'the inherited capital of morality which our forefathers accumulated, and which we only squander instead of increasing'.

In this regard the focus of the reforms is not the community realizing, as Morris would have it, *the best life for itself*; it is rather the individual realizing the best *deal* for him/herself. Schools are encouraged to see themselves as independent businesses developing their own individual characters and ethos; this outside of local political control if they choose grant-maintained status. It is the ethos and performance of individual schools upon which the sum total of the public good rests, rather than underlying aims for society as a whole. Thus, the reforms both reflect the privatization of values which is a phenomenon of our age, and exacerbate the loss of corporate overview.

The silent market machine

The question for the management of schools is how far common social and educational values are shared and can find expression in our market-place society today, as I explored in an article for *Success*, the Journal of the Centre for the Study of Comprehensive Schools (CSCS):

> The twentieth century has seen a disintegration of conventional and traditional authority and morality and we have not yet formulated the possibilities of a new order. Internalised habits and taboos still guide our behaviour. We are a society in transition, but a society whose technology and pace seem to require certainties and quick decisions rather than delays for contemplation or reflection.
>
> The focus today is on activism, operationalism and instrumentalism, for they are easier to measure and manage. Thus in educational reform, instead of requiring 'that school participants penetrate the level of immediacy of everyday actions and practices of schooling in relation to the social, cultural, political and economic context of education' as Lawrence Angus suggests in ' "New" Leadership and the Possibility of Reform' (1989) we have instead an unproblematic

notion of product which can be watchdogged by the consumer parent, through a greater supposed visibility of performance evidenced through testing and other, still rather indeterminate, performance indicators.

In fact, rather than drawing closer to a common framework of values by 'school participants' we are moving further into the silence of a confused culture, the controlling silences behind a culture which throws up the type of National Curriculum whose lack of rationale John White deplores.

There is the silence of paternalism which pervades society in the nostalgia for the certainties and power levers of a former age; the silence of abstract systems in a modern, technological society; the silence around a common framework of values in an increasingly pluralist society; the silence of myth which harnesses the emotions of a public consciousness untrained in critical thinking and self-awareness; the silence of a divide in our culture between reflection and action; and the silence of a collaborative or corporate ethic in the rugged individualism of modern consumerism (West, 1991, p 26).

Education's role should ideally redeem the silences of our culture: the paradoxes and ambiguities which we, in our anxiety to tie up loose ends, tend to ignore and overlook in the comfort of theories and ideologies which often have little to do with real life on the ground.

The silences of our transitional culture contain the issues which need to be addressed. They are not deliberately suppressed through tyranny or conspiracy: they are suppressed rather by a lack of time or will to reflect on questions of value and a reliance on concepts like market forces which provide an escape from such reflection and personal and collective responsibility.

The market as determinant of education is a far cry from Matthew Arnold, the Victorian educator and poet who saw education as the bastion of culture: the study of perfection in order to perfect the world:

The disparagers of culture make its motive curiosity; sometimes, indeed, they make its motive mere exclusiveness and vanity ... There is a view in which all the love of our neighbour, the impulses towards action, help, and beneficence, the desire for removing human error, clearing human confusion, diminishing human misery, the noble aspiration to leave the world better and happier than we found it – motives eminently such as are called social – come in as part of the grounds of culture, and the main and pre-eminent part ... *it is a study of perfection* ... And because men are all members of one great whole ... Perfection, as culture conceives it, is not possible while the individual remains isolated. The individual is required, under pain of being stunted and enfeebled in his own development if he disobeys, to carry others along with him in his march towards perfection ... perfection [is] an *inward* condition ... at variance with the mechanical and material civilisation in esteem with us (Arnold, 1932, pp 44-9).

We have a problem in our sceptical age with such language: it strikes us as rather romantic and not rooted in practical applications. We need an inclusiveness where the ideal is not at variance with the mechanical and material but instead of establishing a new language, we allow ourselves to move into the silence of markets and machinery. Our flight into the mechanistic and technocratic, however, does not denote a flight from value, but rather a flight from the *expression* of value.

This notwithstanding, without efforts on the part of our educational institutions to give our individual and common aspirations credible voice, we shall drown in operational and activist silence.

Schools which succumb thoughtlessly to such machinery are compounding our general confusion. Though under considerable pressure to do so, schools must not resort to peddling value packages and image-making in their concern to attract customers, but must find ways to affirm a moral responsibility to promote critical thinking and a renewal of collaborative purpose. This is not to say that this is an easy challenge for school leadership nor that there will not be elements of compromise. The school is nevertheless the most obvious vehicle to promote an examination of a cultural and community agenda; it also has the right human scale to do so effectively.

A shared responsibility

Whether schools are compelled to compound the silences of our culture or whether, even in their new market position, they can act as a remedial influence is the central reflection and directional thrust of this book. The fact is that in any circumstance there is room for some manoeuvre. Though the service has become increasingly circumscribed in terms of centrally directed organizational constraints and

27

value-emphasis, there is, nevertheless, in the devolving of powers to the schools, a potential for a more locally rooted framework of values and responsibilities.

The White Paper (1992) emphasizes two major influences on the school's ethos and quality – that of the head in creating an ethos and that of parents in endorsing that ethos in their choice of school. Dependent on such popular approval it is possible for heads to imagine that their job is to pander to the public, creating images and signals which are designed to promote what they think the parents want and to dazzle parents into assent. Indeed, the reaction is understandable when the Government says in its Paper that parents 'know ... better than educational theorists ... administrators ... and our mostly excellent teachers' (p 2).

This, however, is a defeatist and victim position which does not support the role of schools as educative community centres. It betrays not only the public which deserves more leadership and respect, but it betrays also the professional voice which has a very significant contribution to make. Educational leadership must be able to articulate a well-thought-out educational philosophy which allows for other voices and questions and does not resort to cliché, glib assertion or unexamined statement.

Such professional leadership has a clear idea of where it is going and is able to share its vision with others confidently and positively; it is not afraid to face questions and doubts about its aims or objectives. It is prepared and able to examine values and to share questions with others, recognizing that such a process gains more than silent assent: it gains partners, friends, allies, informed supporters and even the possibility of an educated public and more integrated community.

Thus, schools can either retreat from such scrutiny or pressure or they can harness it for their own good and, perhaps more idealistically, the good of the education service as a whole. To state such a possibility is not to underestimate the task facing heads and their governing bodies in the new scenario, for what constitutes a good school varies from person to person, all of whom have been to schools themselves and all of whom have a notion of what schools should be like. One has only to own up at any social event to being a teacher for that to be quite apparent. If one adds this to the plurality of values already mentioned of a multi-faith and faithless society, any possibility of straightforward consensus on what constitutes a good education for each and every child becomes even more problematic.

Controversies – minor and major

The leadership model outlined above is relatively comfortable with controversy and anticipates it sensibly rather than allowing it to creep up unannounced. Rather than energy spent avoiding conflict at all costs, the leadership envisaged learns to live with it and to deal with its more public face. Popular image-making, of course, is one way of keeping the conflicts of potentially disparate values at bay. However, controversies do and will occur whatever efforts are made to avoid them, as the various disputes between either heads and governors or heads and parents reported in the local and national press demonstrate. Heads are particularly vulnerable, for governors will be guided by the head but their support may be undermined if the policies advocated do not meet with the parents' approval. State sector heads will be subject to similar pressures as those of fee-paying schools: the customer is likely to be right.

David Hart, the general secretary of the National Association of Headteachers, pointed out in the *Guardian*, 6 June 1992, in relation to a GMS school in Stratford, London, where the head's authority was threatened by ethnic controversy engendered from the governing body itself, that such controversy must not be viewed 'as ... unique ... there are other schools which currently have similar disputes, albeit of a more minor nature'. Indeed, a controversy which had some coverage in the Cambridge local press revolved around a school dropping Latin from the timetable.

The relationships which are created by a leadership which is able to anticipate conflict by meeting it positively up-front rather than covertly, if this is at all possible, are more likely to withstand any potential conflict. Such a climate is likely to be more robust to allow for differences to be resolved. Siege produces attack and attack produces siege: the management of the 1990s needs to pre-empt cycles of conflict developing by moving towards sources of perceived opposition before hostilities break out. School leaders need to manage *values* not crises born of silence.

Management of values

Yet values in management and school leadership have been a neglected area in the development programmes of aspiring and practising heads; it has also not figured to any great extent in the even patchier training of governors. Management theory in recent years has tended to focus on the 'technocracy' of management, ie the tendency to focus solely on technical and operational issues, and there is a need, particularly now, where corporate values are becoming more invisible, to bring educational thinking back to the 'why and wherefore' of schools, in order that the 'how' be more strategically thought out and effected. Management skills must incorporate strategic and organizational competencies, but the latter cannot effectively *precede* a focus on values, or decisions become blind and headless. Values which are not harnessed to strategy and realism are equally impotent: good management is an interactive dynamic between both aspects, but the process has to start with an awareness of the values which figure both as a reality and as a possibility at the micro level of the school, within the macro level of the wider community. Heads who wish to manage their schools without reference to this greater dimension are deliberately putting blinkers on themselves and, more seriously, on the eyes of their school communities.

It has been, and still is, important for aspiring and practising heads to concentrate on the craft of management, however, if they wish to accept the mantle of responsibility which Morris and Arnold wished to place on their shoulders in terms of a cultural mission for the community school, they also need to become professionally skilled in the management of values. It is not a question of school leaders seizing any high moral ground in their management of schools, but of their enabling understanding and consideration in their school communities of cultural and ethical issues, allowing others to develop and exercise their own leadership skills appropriately. This approach enables all touched by the school to breach inarticulacy and inertia and to realize the best life for themselves and each other, by requiring that the value context of the goals are understood, and that initiatives to action are governed by commitment to the value of those goals. Tasks then become choices of value which engage initiative and commitment.

The leadership of thinking teams

This reflective leadership develops people and teams in a more multi-dimensional way, making individuals and groups thoughtful agents of improvement and change. Through a common understanding and shared experience of value questions and dilemmas, more fertile and negotiated strategies can emerge which, because of a real involvement in responsibility, build a strong bonding of the group or community. In relation to what has been said earlier of the silence and fragmentation of modern culture and society, such leadership has enormous implications for any possible restoration of a collaborative ethic through communities working together and redefining their purposes. David Marquand describes this working ethic in *The Unprincipled Society* (1988, p 233) thus:

> The leader is neither charismatic hero, carrying salvation in his saddle bags, nor technocratic manager pushing through an objectively 'correct' solution. He or she is a kind of pastor or moderator or chairman – if possible, wiser and more experienced than the rest of us, and as such entitled to respect, but with no special technical knowledge and no pretensions to heroism – whose role is to set off the learning process, to bring us face to face with the contradictions in our values and, if possible, to elicit latent consensus.

Such common understanding and commitment are highly desirable for schools in any circumstances, but in the more autonomous and isolated situation in which they are likely to find themselves, the ability to enable group interaction and cohesion becomes more than desirable, it becomes an essential competence. The leadership of schools has to deal with stakeholders of the school – parents, students, staff, governors, and the wider community – more directly and make of disparate parts a greater whole if they are to enjoy some consensus of confidence and support. It is not likely, or even desirable, that dissidence will be eradicated but, as more freely floating vessels, schools will need the fairest of following winds, and this means their community must be a committed crew.

The exhortation, therefore, in the reforms, that parents and the community should have a major say in our schools, should be welcomed and professionally managed rather than the subject of dismay. The management task of the 1990s in schools is to provide whatever bulwarks it can for the reintegration of corporate spirit and sense in the greater dislocation of society today. The poet Rainer Maria Rilke, in his monograph on Rodin, talks of his sculptural fragments being expressive of the whole – a hand expressive of a body and soul. In their fragmented status today schools can try to do the same through opening to themselves and their stakeholders the various questions and dilemmas of education, rather than selling them packaged images. In so doing they will be engaging the community in participation, relationship and self-government which is more constructive than passive assent, helpless dependency or silent exit. In managing diversity/fragmentation heads and governors are managing values. Their willingness to engage with those values, and their skills in doing so, are vital to an integration of value and voice as opposed to conflict and exit, and it is with their capacity to achieve this integration that the following chapter is concerned.

Chapter 2

The Head as Influence Agent

Defensiveness and demand

The new emphasis on parent power, whether real or apparent, has developed a sense of siege in many heads and teachers who seem called upon to right every ill in society as if they were personally responsible for them. They are called upon, too, to respond to every diverse need often without any reference to their human capacity or resource to do so. This unquenchable demand, coupled with a distrust of professional influence and the greater powers assigned to governors and parents, has led some heads to a determination either to satisfy popular demands or to become a closet liberal or radical, keeping the hordes at bay, as it were. In this chapter I shall be looking at four possible modes of a head's influence. This is not to suggest that there will be four distinctive types of head, for every head may exercise one or more of these modes at some point. For the purposes of clarity, however, I will refer to four discrete modes. These are:

1 *Reactive headship* – this is where the head identifies either totally or cynically with perceived popular values. In other words, whatever parents appear to want from a school the head endeavours to provide. The reactive head does not believe that schools shape and transform a society but that they only reflect that society. Reactive headship reinforces the status quo.

2 *Closet headship* is where the head does not entirely identify with popular values but is willing to put up enough of a façade of convention that parents will not be unduly alarmed by any

experiment or innovation. This head prefers to keep a low profile and subverts tradition from the back, as it were, slipping in more progressive methods gently.

3 *Oasis headship* – this where the head has value-congruence internal to the school but has not necessarily been able or concerned to convince the customers. Under the new competitive arrangements where the camel trains might find other watering holes, the school has either to go out and seek custom for its particular assets or face a shrinking clientele.

4 *The proactive head* is one who is prepared to come up-front with his or her values and attempts to involve parents more in the debate. It is not simply a question of selling certain ideas, for this might also happen with modes 1 and 2. It is more a question of allowing the 'laity' to understand more of the complexities and sharing with them the ideas behind those complexities. This is a shaping and educative mode.

Some examples from the survey give an insight into the four modes of emphasis and the relative advantages and disadvantages of these styles.

1 A longer fuse

One head of long standing described how he had learnt the job through doing it; he recognized that new heads would have had more management science and training than he had done but was sceptical that such skills could be taught. His first task in taking office was to move the school into the comprehensive stage; it had formerly been a secondary modern and he had to convince parents that his school could provide what the grammar school would have done. He also had to woo doubtful parents away from the private sector:

HEAD: We did start off very much as a Grammar Secondary Modern purely to win the parents over ... we didn't stream, we setted rigidly, we still do – that's what the parents wanted.

SW: How did you pick that up, that that's what they wanted?

HEAD: It's the nature of the catchment area, a lot of professional people. We've done very well in stemming the flow of people from us to the private sector. In fact it works the other way now ... you can count on one hand the number we lose to the private sector.

Having established the academic credibility of the school, the head had carried on in very much the same vein ever since, making adjustments to the curriculum and organization very gently as the need presented itself. The head identified with the parents' wishes but saw it as the professionals' job to make decisions about the child's learning. This was evident in his response to parental queries over setting:

sw: Do you pick up any elements ... of [parental] worry about kids not being in top sets?

HEAD: Not so much now; we used to suffer from that. *They thought they decided which sets the children went into* (my italics).

sw: Is it the case that you would say on the whole you as head, and probably most of the staff, identify with what the parents want, rather than feeling what they want is against your principles?

HEAD: I think that's very true that I put the parents' wishes and views before mine.

The head's belief in non-interference from the 'laity' was reinforced by his perception of their interest in school organization and curricula. He had seen no evidence of parents and governors wanting to be more involved:

HEAD: I don't know that the parents really want to do that and this idea that parents and governors should be more involved, I don't see a lot of that. They want to know what's going on, but they don't necessarily want to be involved. They're quite happy to leave it to the professionals, as long as professionals are doing it the way they want it done.

He went on to acknowledge that they had been slow to respond to some needs because there was no discernible demand from the customers. Special Needs provision, for example, had only really been introduced five years previously:

HEAD: I would think in the last five years we've perhaps given more emphasis to the lower end of the spectrum. Perhaps at the beginning we neglected that because there wasn't the pressure from outside for us to do it and, again, with the sort of catchment area we've got we don't have a big problem. Now the danger with that is, if you haven't got a big problem you ignore it altogether, and I think we may have been guilty of that.

sw: Is that the danger of the customer-driven approach?

HEAD: That's right, because it's going to be the parents with the more able children that'll call the tune. If you're not careful you neglect [those] who don't shout and they tend to be the lower ability children.

Generally the head felt schools had to respond to change rather than initiate changes. The media, he felt, had more influence on children than the school. He was not, however, entirely without some hope of influence:

HEAD: It is more difficult for an individual head to have their own values ... If they've got them it's harder for them to impose them, because really I think that the days where the head was the figure-head of the school, and what he or she said went, I mean those days are gone. I mean your head today is very much a cajoler, a facilitator, a listener for bringing along the people ... I suppose implicit in that is that your values are coming through. But you're not out there to bring everyone along behind you. You're in there with them, sort of bringing them along the way you want to go.

Not only had the head had to change his management style but he had also to push some of his staff on. Sixty per cent of the staff had been in the school for more than ten years. It was a comfortable and gently moving environment, whose pace now had to change as the map of education was changing around the school. The head realized as he contemplated retirement that his style of headship was now being replaced by a more trained breed of heads; he also recognized that his style would not fit all eventualities:

HEAD: I think if I was head of a school in the middle of an inner city, I would run it totally differently. I don't know that my type of headship ... would fit in with that; I don't think I could do the job, to be quite honest. But there you would have to have more of your own philosophy ... because there's not anything coming in from outside. There's not the support from interest in education as there is in the catchment like this.

2 An understated influence
Another head interviewed had taken on a similarly rather traditional school which had blazers, formal assemblies and a prefect system – in many ways the type of school whose values might accord with parents'

own schooldays and expectations. The head decided to keep these signals in place, for to ban them suddenly was likely to alarm parents and make them doubt his own competence as a head. He had no wish to rock the boat though his own personal values were at variance with the ethos and expectations which these traditional signals represented. He decided to adopt a 'softly, softly' approach in liberalizing the regime and he did this discreetly and gently. First of all, he did not want the children to stand up when he came into Assembly, and he spent a whole summer, he admitted, working this one out. On returning in the September he ensured that he was always in Assembly before the children and thus there was no need for them to stand up. He changed the title of prefects to 'senior students', elected by their peers rather than appointed, and altered their role to be more supportive of students with less policing, and he left the blazers in place.

He felt he had to live with some of the traditional expectations of the catchment though the attitudes saddened him:

> HEAD: I figure the worst thing I could do ... would be to make any indication of getting rid of blazers and ties because of the super-ficiality [of parents] ... saddens me I suppose ... if the uniform's good and the children are polite then it must be a good school ... if we want to make any progress on the curriculum ... we can only do that behind the façade of blazers and ties.

I suggested that the head had decided to leave some mechanisms in place in order to get on with other, perhaps more important, matters. Nevertheless, as the medium is also the message these compromises were never insignificant. The head agreed but acknowledged that there were some things he could live with and some he was not prepared to live with. It was a matter of compromise and understated influence.

The one thing, for example, he could not live with, and he altered immediately, was a custom in the staffroom of making children the subject of jokes which were pinned on the notice-board: this he simply banned. Each year in writing the School Development Plan the curriculum was becoming slightly more innovative and radical so that his values were prevailing, albeit in a context of some compromise, but no sudden change of direction worried staff, parents or students. The ability of this head to manoeuvre forward within quite traditional expectations contrasted with the agony of another head whose principles were at variance with popular expectations. The parents of his traditional catchment were voting with their feet: his roll was dropping.

3 A tension of principles and compromise

This head faced the adverse effect of popular values in that his school, which had abandoned uniform 12 years previously, was faced with open enrolment and was losing out to more traditional schools in the area. There were other factors to do with area and academic results which might have counted in the equation but the head and staff were beginning to agonize over whether they should change their corporate values, which might well alienate those parents who made a positive choice of the school because of what it stood for. A slight shift had taken place towards academe in acknowledging staff qualifications in their brochure but the head was not happy to compromise the school's principles further:

> HEAD: We are here to educate students, not to provide teachers with jobs, or not, when it boils down to it, to do what parents want necessarily ... it seems to me that if one has [a concern for] that centrality of the students, I don't regard the uniform issue as an insignificant one. If I say to them, you are young people, you are not children, it is your education and we want you to take decisions – but I am going to tell you what to wear every morning...

This head had chosen the school very carefully because it embodied his own values. Rather like the first head cited, he did not see himself fitting into every school setting. I teased this idea out with him:

> sw: You came into a particular situation where you identified with qualitative management issues surrounding a negotiated code of values. But another head may be entering a completely run-down situation.
> HEAD: I think this relates so strongly to the 'horses for courses' issue I referred to, and self-knowledge. I wouldn't want to say that I lack the ability to do a different sort of job, but I think there is a balance in us – the balance of our temperament and our professional expertise. You are less likely to be effective if the demands of the job do not match your particular skills and temperament.

This head was not at all sure he really wanted to compromise with the views of parents outside the school. Internally the school ran with almost total value congruence: the governors were in tune with its ethos, the students were happy and well-behaved, the LEA had supported it in the past because the values were applauded. Suddenly, however, the school found itself no longer under the protection of the LEA: staff and resources had had to be cut as LMS removed discretionary resourcing. The introduction of open enrolment and parental choice meant that the people now to convince of the school's values were no longer the professionals or governors but the unpredictable public. Lines of communication to parents were not strong despite efforts to get them involved. A hesitation lay nevertheless in the head's reluctance to expose the ideals of the school to a potentially fickle market place. He mused almost to himself that to change a school's character to satisfy superficial and ill-thought-out popular values was a heresy not devoutly to be wished:

HEAD: Say [a school] was to be closed down, and it represented a certain set of values. If in order to maintain it you had to change it beyond all recognition and have an entirely different and perhaps alien set of values simply in order to maintain that school, [and here the thought became too distasteful to contemplate] then there is a view that because a school is good and appropriate, that justifies maintaining it at all costs and for all time.

The emotional reaction to having to corrupt principles that this head held dear would not allow him to move beyond his absolute belief in the school's character. However, the challenge remained of how the parents might be convinced of this good. I left him with the dilemma still to work out. There would have been no guarantee that introducing uniform, for example, would attract more parents but the control of the market place means that convictions must be communicated persuasively to parents if we are to enlist their vote. If this head wishes to stick to his convictions then he needs to find ways to overcome the parental doubts which keep them from choosing his school.

In the same way that the reactive head doubted that schools can actually influence society, the third head cited did not have faith in the impact of ideas either but exercised them only within the safe confines of a sheltered situation. The school had had buffers in the past and in that situation had become complacent, perhaps, about the rights and perceptions of parents. Passivity may have been taken for assent. In today's climate that assent has to be worked for. Too many heads see the choice as being purely between total surrender to popular values or holding the ignorance of the public 'out there' back. This is insular and patronizing; it is also the abandonment of the idea that voice is still a persuasive tool. The market is seen as a machine which has greater power than human mission and message. Such lying down to the inevitable hardly constitutes a good message to the young. No head could be said to have solutions to hand but it is important to be at least working on them.

The head is no longer simply building a team of staff and pupils; s/he is also *pivotal* in building a parent and community team which also includes the governing body. Not only is the governing body an important team in the making of policy and guardianship of the school, but the parents are a further team to be built up as friends and watchdogs of all that is dear and important in their children's education. Parents become more involved and develop more understanding of the school's aims where their children are also involved and enthusiastic about their learning and school experiences. Heads and teachers will need to consider these teams more carefully in the future if some corporate sense is to be achieved. If schools are the educative centres of our community, and in our increasingly secularized world it is imperative that they are, then they have to deal with that community. Some schools have a harder challenge than others but all schools need parental confidence and support; but this is the subject of a later chapter.

In terms of reactive, closet or oasis headship the heads were choosing to exert an influence in a rather *covert* or independent sort of way, and in the case of the last head this was not producing the degree of parental confidence to ensure the security of the roll. The problem with covert influence is that it does not easily harness understanding and participation which schools in their more autonomous position today need to do. One may find, therefore, that one is presiding over a school whose integrity and principles are wholly intact but which does not convince the outside world. There may be little wrong with the principles; it is the strategies for engendering confidence that may need reconsideration. However ambivalent the head may feel about going to the parents there are times when more proactive measures are needed.

4 A bolder stroke

The fact remains that the head of an establishment has to seek to be the influence and change agent of his or her institution through being clear about the values and direction s/he wants to take, articulating this and harnessing the support of staff, governors, students and particularly parents to it. The focus must move from analysis to proactive strategies applicable to the circumstances of the school. This had been the attitude and approach of another head who harnessed loyalty through openness and participation. The school was situated in a working-class area of a new town. At the time of his appointment to the school as head, confidence locally had been at a low ebb and the roll had been falling. In 18 months he had, however, established new confidence sufficiently for the roll to be rising. I asked him how up-front he had been about his own values:

SW: We are particularly interested in the competencies which attach to managing an educational philosophy ... how far should heads be up-front with their own values ... Did you at any stage ... come out and say, 'I stand for this'?

HEAD: Yes, I think I started from that point, because I thought that was right. I made through bulletins, at interviews, at public meetings, a number of unequivocal statements about what I stood for ... Things such as 'a good school must be an orderly school'. That doesn't mean to say that discipline has to be harsh, but I think there have to be rules and regulations that are clearly articulated, clearly understood, but within that there is an atmosphere which is supportive ... I was clear about boundaries. Another area was that I value examination results; whether we like it or not that is the system we have, and our job is to help the children to get the best possible GCSE results, not by whatever means, but by learning that is exciting and interesting, but there may be times when it is not ... there may be a time when chalk and talk is the appropriate method ... But I also want to see within a talking curriculum lots of different ways of learning. So I said all this. I think the kids, as individuals, have a right to be heard. They are the primary reason we are here. So in terms of values, we value them.

To back up the emphasis on learning the head had introduced a system of systematic department reviews and work reviews where each child's progress was discussed with the child and family. I probed him further on this back up of the rhetoric:

> HEAD: We invite the families for a half-hour work review where we just talk about academic matters ... For ... Years Ten and Eleven ... the team is myself, the deputies, senior teachers and the Head of Year. We work attached to a tutor group, so I have a tutor group ... We have a two month period in which we have got to complete 20 interviews each. This is fundamental ... in ... ensuring that pupils have every opportunity to achieve their best. So if we say to the pupil that he is not doing enough homework ... the parents can say, 'Well, the head said you must do two hours', which has more impact than a letter, which would be ignored.

Beyond the internal reviews and his public statements of values, the head had issued a questionnaire to all stakeholders – staff, governors, parents and students – about their likes and dislikes about the school and their concerns. The results had been considered by staff, students and governors and some changes brought in. He had also instituted an Open Day for parents who could come in to see the school actually running; he and the senior team ran morning surgeries and he had appointed a public relations officer who was responsible among other things for a weekly newsletter to parents where any and every event was celebrated and reported, including my visit. The head had also undertaken to keep governors up to date with a news-sheet which carried the dialogue and decisions of the sub-committees for all governors.

It was evident that very little was hidden from governors and parents: they were all in the enterprise together. His chair of governors was enthusiastic and fully supported the school. She related as a parent governor her pride in the school:

> We are very lucky here in that our whole governing body has a very open relationship with [head's Christian name] and the staff. It is our school ... we discuss everything. It's not all done as senior management. We wanted to find out how parents, pupils, governors, staff felt about the school. And he has only been here a year. He's done a lot. So we put a survey out to everybody, asking them to tell us what was good ... what was bad, what they were not happy about, and we got an overall picture ... We brought in an actual ... PE kit with their own logo and a black V-neck jumper ... more

formality ... Then in our weekly bulletin that we send out we set out the main points that had been picked up, and what we were doing about them, and how the pupils felt ... we have a PR and Marketing Director ... in our open weeks ... [we] invite the local community into the school.

The power of ideas

The four schools described above had very different catchment areas and expectations but the involvement of parents in the last school cited was positively sought and harnessed. The danger of the more reactive and intuitive response, while understandable in a stable and relatively satisfied catchment, is that certain aspects of childrens' needs and unheard parental voice can be overlooked. Covert influence, too, may at times be the better part of valour, but opportunities can be missed to educate a community and to build on their commitment and goodwill. It is only through heads and communities examining values and practice in a planned and systematic way that real quality and individual attention will occur. The consideration of a dynamic educational philosophy and dynamic strategies for the realization of that philosophy, albeit within the constraints of whatever political and social framework in which the school has to operate, is going to become increasingly, in a competitive and publicly accountable climate, a central competency in school leadership and management.

Schools should be *suggesting the ideas* not reacting to them only. School leadership has to move from operationalism and reaction to the open promotion of ideas. Covert influence is not enough. It may feel safer for a time to keep one's head below the parapet but it will not serve for the whole battle. Reactive, closet or oasis headship must give way to forms of management which encourage appraisal of the school by stakeholders.

Peter Abbs (1979, p 3) expresses very well the attitudinal shift we must make in management:

We severely underestimate the power of philosophical ideas in this country, and try to turn the deficiency into a strength by elevating the tendency 'to muddle through' into a superior and exclusive way of life ... when moral, existential and cultural confusion is so everywhere apparent, our fear of intellectual conception and philosophical argument is nothing less than a vice, for it is a habit which binds us, inexorably, to accepting an unacceptable status quo … It is true that social realities affect ideas, but the contrary is also the case: ideas have the power to affect realities, even to create them.

Heads must stand back sufficiently from the day-to-day, and though besieged by the platitudes and simplistic attitudes of the media and some politicians, it will not suffice to go to ground or to become complacent. Heads need to stand up for what they believe in and those who do, more often than not, find that parents respect their views and, indeed, are often quite relieved to hear certain convictions expressed, though they may well want their chance to comment on or modify those views. In contrast to the first head's belief that heads are less influential than they used to be, I believe they are just as influential as they ever were, provided that they do have some values and beliefs to communicate. I asked one head whether she felt she did carry such weight?

HEAD: Yes, more than I probably realize … I suppose I do not fully acknowledge or realize, especially in a smallish community, just how significant the head's beliefs are.

That heads, therefore, have the potential to be influence agents is evident. How far they should and do exercise that influence relates to circumstances in the field and their own perception of their right to any influence. There are dangers as well as benefits in such influence, of course, for there is still in the pivotal role of the head the opportunity for him or her to be very narrow and dogmatic, without there being necessarily any formally constituted challenge or assessment of an intellectually rigorous kind to qualify that stance. Heads are at liberty to continue to run tight ships and not to stir from the purely operational arena in their thinking. However, their schools and communities are most probably the poorer, for the thinking school is one where ruts and complacent habits are more likely to be avoided, though experiment and innovation bring their risks, too.

With the responsibility for appointing heads now falling to governing bodies, with possibly no professional influence, the probability of heads being chosen for all manner of local and parochial reasons may grow. Clearly there is a necessity to establish professionally recognized development programmes for heads where aspiring and practising heads are encouraged to examine their own values and stock of strategies carefully. Such programmes would develop skills also in how heads might involve the other stakeholders in the enterprise. Rather as a doctor is trusted to judge how much a patient really ought (or wishes) to know of his malady, heads are judging the receptiveness and capacities of their communities. It is a fact, however, that the movement in today's world is away from paternalism and towards information to the patient or parent/student, whether they can handle that positively or negatively.

Despite all the problems raised by influence, leadership will be needed, not in seizing necessarily any high moral ground, but in not being afraid to hold beliefs and, where conscience dictates, to persuade others, if at all possible, of the importance of those beliefs. In doing this, one must recognize, as David Marquand puts it in *The Unprincipled Society* (1988, p 245), 'that although no-one could pretend that it would be easy to reach consensus in any circumstances, it is more likely to come through power sharing and negotiation than any other way'.

Heads must have more confidence in their own ideas and cultivate those ideas. They must recognize that well-thought-out philosophy and values are still a potent force in society; indeed, they are probably the most important force in our increasingly atomized, individualistic and dislocated society. For this reason they require more explicit professional attention.

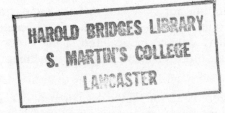

Chapter 3

The Professional College and Educative Leadership

The loss of shared ideas and networks

The move in the last decade or so to focus on the techniques of management both at classroom and whole school levels has left a gap in matters of the moral and social purposes of schools in teacher and headteacher training. Sir William Taylor, in his Peterson Lecture (1990, p 4), characterized it thus:

> One of the duties of the director of the Oxford Department was to deliver a lecture course on the ideas of the Great Educators – in the Mulcaster Room named after one of Oxford's own. Such courses now seldom feature in programmes of initial teacher training. There is little time for close study of the famous texts of our trade. I understand well enough why they have been squeezed out. There are many skills to be acquired in the all too short year of post-graduate professional training. But something of value has been lost in the process.

It is squeezed out, too, in the development of heads not only through the greater pragmatism and expediency which has crept into the whole service but by the fact that it has never formally figured in any head's training. When a greater consciousness arose that heads needed professional training, the focus tended to be on the managerial aspects only, which were considered to be the greatest deficit areas in educational management compared with industry. Of course, the great ideas of education have been kept alive through all sorts of professional networks and informal contacts and influences but in today's more fragmented service the networks and influences need to be cultivated more deliberately by the profession if quality and excellence in terms of vision and practice are to be disseminated and maintained. Most heads interviewed saw such a focus on ideas and contact as their lifeblood. When asked about their own educational values most responded readily with heartfelt views, though they appeared unused to expressing them. It was suggested to one head that the new emphasis on managerialism did not provide practice for the expression of values or inspiration for aspiring heads and, in the selection of heads, such concerns might often be secondary to management technique. The head replied:

> I think that is quite sad. In fact, I wonder what sustains you in being a head and in running a school if you do not have that inner belief and that inner vision, because it is a mighty rough mountainside that you are climbing, and unless you have those golden dreams at the top (some of which you may modify, some of which you may never achieve), unless you have them there, it is a heavy path to tread if you do not know why. I find people who cannot give me that sort of vision and inspiration rather let me down. A lot of people are like this who are in key positions in education, and I find that quite depressing.

Certainly the practice of such vision and dialogue has not been easy to maintain in today's world across the service; there was disappointment for example that LEAs either had never shown leadership in this respect, or, where they had, that this was now overtaken by practical dilemmas or pragmatics. One head described the change in one LEA which had had a reputation for progressive and enlightened thinking. When he joined the authority, however, he found, because of legislative reforms, 'it was very much contemplating its navel, and moving from a philosophical basis to an almost too mechanistic administrative basis. [They] sharpened up and tidied up the administration, maybe at the expense of the esoteric.'

Nevertheless, this head still saw salvation in the 'professional college' that the LEA could and still did, he felt, provide:

HEAD: One came thinking one was entering something special, and indeed one was ... you became part of a special 'club', a professional college, for want of a better phrase, whereby you were mixing fairly regularly with some very inspired people, inspired educators, and the pay-off there was that they were helping me in my development and I was contributing to the growth of the whole.

sw: If you hadn't had the LEA backing you with this 'professional college' you would actually have found it much more tiring to sustain your vision?

HEAD: Personally, yes. I think I would go so far as to say that I would have collapsed inwards, in one sense. It depends on how gregarious you are as an individual, but the thought of being bottled up just inside the institution, albeit with a very challenging and capable senior team, and other colleagues around, I think I would have found difficult ... This is why I keep coming back to the notion of a 'professional college', that that is what sustains people. It is a two-way process. You need to contribute to it and it contributes to your own development. Not only development in a professional, material sense, but in terms of your own revitalization and re-energizing.

Ideas and networks

Of course, not all Authorities have lived up to such professional expectations and in some instances the LEA was experienced simply as a thorough nuisance, invading school agendas with perceived irrelevancies so that some heads just wished to be free of their interference:

HEAD: I am very anti-LEA at the moment, because the LEA is just a burden round one's neck. They even try to dictate the agenda for governors' meetings; you find ... so much of their time is taken up discussing the LEA curriculum policy, that there is not time enough to talk about things that are more pertinent and relevant to us.

It is clear then that not all LEAs, nor all schools for that matter, have consistently provided vision which nourishes and sustains for a variety of reasons. It may be a lack of such vision, ie a restricted professionalism which never rises to the broader view of education, or it may be that some LEAs or schools find themselves so overwhelmed with the practical changes brought in by the Government's reforms, or other such demands, that they lose sight of any wider perspective.

However, there is no doubt that there is a hunger for ideas and the sharing of ideas and, if the profession is to be fragmented further, as seems likely through the breakdown of LEAs, then such atomization has the seeds of both disaster and opportunity. There is a need not to lose sight of the 'professional college' and, indeed, as supplement to a poverty of ideas in either the school or LEA, or both, extended professionals at all levels have always sought, and will no doubt continue to seek, to keep themselves inspired and alive through a variety of networks such as the Centre for the Study of the Comprehensive School (CSCS), the Programme for Reform in Secondary Education (PRISE), the National Association for Values in Education and Training (NAVET), and the Community Education Association (CEA), to name but a few. The various teacher and headteacher associations also play their part and movements such as TANEA (Towards a New Education Act) and the ongoing question of a General Teaching Council are endeavouring to keep alive the professional sense of the way forward. There are, too, the Arts lobbies and research groups as well as subject panels attached to examination boards and so on. It is a fragmented picture but the *cumulative* influence and voice of these organizations should not be underestimated. It is also one, as I shall emphasize in due course, which needs to extend beyond a concept of a purely *professional* 'college' to one that includes the wider community.

Collegial values and cumulative debate

In today's climate it is easy to imagine that there is no time for the wider debate on educational values or simply to become pessimistic about any possibility of collegiality within the service. However, rather than succumbing to such pessimism or apathy, it has to be recognized that the potential for fragmentation in our present systems makes an effort towards collegiality and cumulative debate all the more important. In *Managing the Secondary School* (1985), David Trethowen characterizes good management as the ability to rise far enough above a situation to see it, rather than becoming lost in it. This is no less true because in today's circumstances that situation is more complex than ever.

How this works out in practice at local level will very much depend on local history and experience. Where unity and sympathy have existed pre-GMS, this will not necessarily disappear post-GMS. To see all LEAs as white knights in terms of their having promoted collegiality or educational debate is to distort the situation, and to imagine also that local loyalties and traditions must needs be wiped out overnight is to simplify matters considerably. Collegiality has never rested entirely with LEAs or schools: it has rested on the quality of the individuals who work within them. Thus there is no reason to suppose that those individuals will not emerge in more informal frameworks or that they will not influence others to think beyond the dictates of pure self-interest. Leadership in LEAs and schools may have to reconstitute itself but it must assert itself and it will do so to cumulative effect. There is no reason for GMS schools not to maintain collegial links with other schools or even possibly with some LEAs, though only time will tell what shape this new 'professional college' will actually take. In a time of flux, however, what can be held to are the ideas and values of such a 'college': individuals and like-minded groups must keep working towards this end.

The expectations of professionals in counties like my own, Cambridgeshire, have been and are characterized by 50 years of custom and practice. It is heartening, but perhaps not altogether surprising, therefore, that the heads in Cambridgeshire are seeking to hold on to that tradition through voluntary cooperative working. In a recent Cambridgeshire Association of Secondary Heads' discussion paper the following objectives emerged for consideration:

The objective for all of us is:
(a) To keep all schools involved in working with other schools by providing a forum for discussing professional interests;
(b) To develop codes of practice both locally and county wide;
(c) To create an organizational structure on a county basis capable of:
 (i) involving and working with local groups;
 (ii) providing advocacy on resourcing and policy with whatever authorities, funding or regulatory bodies exist or come into existence (2 June 1992).

Certainly there is a touch of universal values there! What is clearly at stake is a determination not to lose sight of a stable and values-driven framework for education. However, such a framework needs also to encourage the support for thinking and reflective schools which inevitably has to start with a thinking head: one who can apply an educational philosophy to practical strategies for action.

Reflection and action

The educator who ceases to educate and stimulate him or herself cannot maintain a vision for others. As I have already stressed, in recent years the training of heads, such as there has been, has focused largely on managerialism which has been helpful in sharpening up management practice in schools. In fact, heads are just as likely now to study for a Masters in Business Administration as a Masters in Education – such has been the shift in emphasis. However, such sharpening of the tools of management still cannot be a substitute for the development of educational ideas and philosophy. If, too, those ideas are to harness collaboration and commitment in the wider community, which is a desirable factor in the silent market today, then schools need to reach out with ideas and projects into that market. The school is no longer a dependent model, fitting into a predictable framework, but is a creative force which establishes networks and creates opportunities to realize its vision.

In the case of my own school, for example, we have been involved for a number of years in integrating pupils with physical disabilities into the mainstream curriculum. Aware of the fragility of finance for such work, the college has adopted a high profile approach to this aspect of Special Needs with media coverage, consultancy work and considerable emphasis on networking. The coordinator of this area has published a series of books on Independence and Integration and as part of a constant research and development approach is now seconded for part of her week to work on the following proposal drawn up in 1991:

It is proposed that a new role of Development Officer should be created for 3 days a week from September 1992. This would be a research and development post and would cover 3 main areas:

- Setting up Impington as a centre for evaluating equipment and advising on integration.
- Extending support for families of children with disabilities (providing the background for a book on working with families).

- Researching into the potential for developing a business enterprise unit for 16+ students with disabilities.

The project coordinator is working closely with other agencies such as social services, the Training and Enterprise Council as well as national and international groups concerned with training and disability. The post has been financed through the coordinator working part of her week on a freelance basis within a part secondment. Through being freed for part of the week, the Development Officer can be released for outreach work in terms of both family support and entrepreneurial scope. It is an entirely new venture with a flexible brief but through working with the vision and enterprise of the teacher involved, the school is working on new opportunities with that member of staff and with the wider community.

The preparedness of the school management to back such vision has to sit within a general belief in making opportunities happen rather than waiting on central frameworks and direction, which in any case are fast disappearing with the demise of LEAs. All schools have inspiring and inspired teachers searching for outlets for their ideas and energies. Leadership is not about one person having a premium on good ideas. It is about encouraging and facilitating the energy of those ideas through a climate which combines reflection and action in creative measure.

Without inspiration, the drive of individuals and the flexible support of institutions, such vision will not be realized. Schools are admittedly more cut off today from Personal Opportunities' budgets, but research and development strategies have to be an integral part of the school's thinking if in this more fragmented culture ideas and innovation are to survive.

Rather than less focus, therefore, being given to educational ideas and values in today's climate, heads need to keep the thinking and innovative impetus of the school alive. Opportunities exist for collaborative work within, between and outside schools, but space has to be created for some staff to forge the networks and contacts. Though budgets are tight, there are possibilities in new styles of contracts, part secondments and creative in-service arrangements to focus schools on reflective action which benefits and enriches the life and experience of the school within a wider community. Heads need to develop greater awareness of, and competence in, ideas/values management, in just the same way that they have developed managerial competences such as curriculum or resources management. First and foremost, however, they must have a vision of what is possible and be able to realize that through a clear appraisal of the actual tools available to them.

The professional centre

In this regard, there is increasingly a need for professional centres for heads to be set up as development and support bases. Development centres like NEAC in Oxfordshire may well be pointing the way forward for other regions. This centre has been engaged in evolving rigorous development and training schemes for headship, tailored to the necessary competences needed in headship which include articulating and implementing an educational philosophy and the management of the actual and potential context of schools.

A backdrop of thinking and creative headship and governance is essential to the potential of the school's educative role and its capacity for anticipating the future rather than being locked into the past. The head's commitment to ideas/values and the facilitating of these are important factors in the training opportunities for all staff, and indeed communities. Working with fellow heads on educational values, competences and strategies in development programmes is an essential opportunity for heads to cooperate and pool ideas and to this end the experience in the USA of Principals' Centres has been very successful, as Roland Barth (1990, pp 84-5) outlines:

When principals learn and share their learning with other principals, they not only feel professional, they become more professional. We see more and more indication that fostering a culture of reflection, learning, cooperation, and professionalism among educators outside their schools contributes to a similar culture among adults and students within schools.

The model which Roland Barth delineates is an applied one; a continuous reflection on practice:

- engage in practice
- reflect on practice
- articulate practice
- better understand practice
- improve practice.

The NEAC development programme now includes exploration of competence in values management: this part of the programme is informed by the outcomes of the Gulbenkian sponsored survey and rests on two key factors. It is an invitation to examine and make explicit the values and philosophy that heads hold – a revealing to themselves and others of what their often assumed values are. It also focuses thinking on the stakeholders in their institution and how far they may contribute to, or hinder, such vision, and therefore what strategies might encourage or mitigate this. The process is termed, in the programme, 'value-mapping'.

Value-mapping

In a culture which is highly pragmatic and unused to the examination of ideas and their application to practice, it is essential in the greater silences of today to practise such examination more deliberately. Thus participants in value-mapping are initially put through a semi-structured questionnaire:

1 What values will you/did you bring to headship?
2 How will you/did you attempt to realize these values in the practice and organization of your school?
3 What helps or hindrances do you expect to meet/did you meet in realizing your educational philosophy? What strategies will you/did you use for dealing with these?
4 How might you/do you involve the various stakeholders in the enterprise, ie staff, governors, pupils, parents and, where appropriate, the LEA?

Similar questions would obtain for chairs of governors, too, who would be involved in the exercise. These personal sessions are followed up by a group session where the outcomes are shared and then a six-month project where participants do sampling interviews of the stakeholders of their own institutions to find out what sort of value-maps obtain in their constituencies. This information is also fed back in groups and reflected upon. The process is as follows:

• analysis of personal and professional values;
• reflection;
• sharing of the personal values perspective with others and the development of strategy thinking;
• Value-mapping exercise involving stakeholders;

- Reflection on findings and further strategy building.

Thus, a thinking head and governing body encourage a thinking and creative school and, with the development of appropriate strategies, a thinking and creative community.

The model of a professional centre for school leaders would provide a forum for ideas to be examined and practice considered. The financing of such a centre in the present climate would require some pooling of resources among schools as well as sponsorship from other sources such as industry, heads' associations and Training and Enterprise Councils. Where there is a common will, however, such technicalities can be worked out. The involvement of governors in value-mapping is an important extension of the 'professional college' and indicates a direction which needs to be further developed in any thinking school.

Research and development

Similarly, to promote research and development in schools the notion of INSET – in-service training – would become increasingly diverse and incorporated into research and development departments, to encourage flexible programmes for staff to pursue projects where the professional development of the teacher and the school's own vision and planning would interact to the benefit of each: a most desirable synergy. Such school-generated projects and programmes are becoming more the norm with devolved training budgets, with departments and institutions of higher education providing more distance learning programmes. Accreditation for Masters in Education can be built up through module credits, with research methods being covered by university supervision with school-based support. The notion of schools having research and development departments dovetails naturally, too, into the Government's plans for more school-based teacher training.

If schools are to be able to support student teachers beyond the techniques and pragmatics of the teacher's role, then the school must have a climate and tradition of applied educational thinking which points to the universal and important questions upon which the daily objectives and tasks of schools are formed. University departments working closely with schools, directed by School Development

Planning, can play a vital part with other sources of development and training in linking teacher skills and self-improvement to experienced teaching, sophisticated thinking and research insight.

The research and development approach also involves teachers, in conjunction with training and research consultants, in supervising development work as well as providing mentoring and monitoring roles for teachers. Such diversification of role will become especially important for teachers' career paths and development, for so many of the jobs which existed outside schools are drying up: extra-school infrastructures such as advisory teacher services are beginning to disappear. Of course, finance has to be found but, again, where such programmes are vision-driven, the school and other potential sponsors may well consider the investment worthwhile. Certainly GMS schools bidding for in-service monies are likely to be basing applications for in-service funding on this combination of whole school direction and the professional development needs of staff.

The research and development department would thus be the values-driven engine of the school, keeping the school under review and directing practice. It would have, too, a role to organize school-based conferences and seminars, which would tap local expertise and thereby provide enrichment for participants and advocacy for the school. These events might also provide some income for the school to finance projects. Certainly such a possibility is built into part of the funding of the Development Officer post, mentioned earlier, and other areas of Impington Village College's focus.

For example, the College has in recent times hosted a number of conferences for organizations such as NAVET and the RSA's regional group, as well as talks and seminars put on by the College as a whole. We also offered the College to the International Baccalaureate Organization (we offer this course in our Sixth Form) for the Modern Language Workshops 1992 and were host to delegates from all over the world. Such conferences have a dual role: they keep alive a sense in the College of the wider issues and world; they also provide a persistent profile for the professionals and non-school professionals who attend them of important value areas of education which get lost sight of in the operationalism of today. For vulnerable areas in terms of educational resourcing such as Special Needs, they bring like-minded people together to sustain each other and strategies to safeguard such provision.

The publication of papers and books on good practice does the same, and teachers generally underestimate not only their expertise but the interest of publishers and other professionals in such reflective practice. Research and development departments then would encourage this profiling and celebration of good practice in the same way that teachers encourage holistic teaching and learning for their pupils. A shorthand model would look like this:

1 A dynamic process of Review and Development.
2 School Development Plan leading to Research/INSET Plan.
3 School based research/development projects.
4 Accreditation through MAs or other relevant validation.
5 Co-supervision – school mentor/researcher consultant.
6 School-based teacher training in conjunction with HE.
7 General INSET, both school-based and off-the-shelf.
8 School centre organized conferences/seminars which will bring in some finance for teacher and management expertise.

Both the professional centre for heads and governors and the research and development department of schools should ensure, in the balance between a values focus and competence training, that there is a corrective to the danger of insularity and complacency of potentially isolated schools, for though Her Majesty's Inspectors have found a direct link between a values-driven school and a clear sense of school purposefulness, they have not found that there is a necessary correlation between successful values and school *effectiveness*. (Green, 1991)

In the market position of schools today, however, it would be tempting for any school which felt it stood for clear values which parents endorse, not to examine its practice too closely. If a formula is a winning one we are all inclined to repeat it. However, as popularizers often find to their cost, formulas can become complacent clichés. In the decentralizing of schools, heads need to provide that critical standback for themselves and their teachers. They need, too, to encourage their governors and parents and pupils to join in that rigour and depth of perspective. The professional centre and research and development department provide essential professional inspiration and discipline which must start, however, with heads examining values, reflecting on practice and involving other stakeholders in the process.

The collective 'professional college'

The thinking school does not confine an examination of values and the excitement of ideas to the professional arena. Governors, parents and pupils need to be encouraged to think about the vision and forward view. Heads and staff need to make the best use of governors' and parents' time and when opportunities arise for contact and interaction the level of focus at which the school pitches its conversations and collaboration is very important. The head, for example, who allows precious governing-body time to focus purely on the minutiae of a financial print-out or on other technical business, is not only mistaking management and policy but losing an opportunity to engage the governing body in the essence of decision-making.

The notion of a 'professional college' (as distinct from the professional centre) has to expand now to that of a collective 'professional college' where governors and parents are encouraged to work through the ideas of education and how they may be applied. Schools in the survey were encouraging governors to think about the School Development Plan rather than just to rubber-stamp it. There was some initial confusion for one governing body, as the interviewee explained. She felt, however, that when governors finally saw the application of the values and principles they benefited from the slight tour into theory:

> I think it has become more and more clear what it is we are about, because when we first saw the notion of a Development Plan quite a number of people on the governors' board commented that it all seemed so vague ... yet when we started to move down the line, as it were, to what were the practical consequences of values of this order, we agreed that we would be giving priority to the quality of the learning experience of the students ... I think the initiative was very much from the executive group on the staff ... there is a kind of rhetoric or vocabulary for this kind of debate, and if you are into it it spills from the tongue very smoothly and very readily, but if you are not, it is really quite a struggle to come to terms with it ... Then to translate it into activities I think helped a great deal.

The model of schools envisaged, therefore, is one that sees itself as mutually educative and dynamic. It will not concentrate on its own internal agenda only but will recognize that its own community can shape the educational agenda, locally, nationally and even inter-nationally. Rather than waiting on leads from elsewhere or some elusive standardized framework, school communities have it in their power to become influence agents themselves and determinants of policy. Such thinking establishments would no doubt wish to maintain networks at all levels of the educational arena and would actively promote an informed and participative community where educational ideas and values are concerned. Such attitudes of outreach, however, must start with the heads being prepared to examine their own values and opening those values to other stakeholders in such a way that critical thought is encouraged. In so doing heads will be pushing out the borders of the 'professional college' aided by the support of rigorous and values-driven programmes of regional professional centres.

Chapter 4

Parent as Stakeholder – Friend or Foe?

The passive consumer

Many heads and governors tend to take parental passivity as a sign of acceptance or even apathy. A number of chairpersons interviewed, for example, were amazed at the low turnout at some functions and really did not feel that the school could do more than offer these opportunities. Assent or apathy, however, may be anything but the case. There are still many inhibiting factors why parents do not choose to offer an opinion or make a fuss and it is always dangerous to take the view of the more vociferous as truly representative. Parental contact with schools often weakens as the children get older and this was borne out in the sample of the survey, with 11-16s and 11-18s still having considerable parental interest compared with the 14-18s and Sixth Form College.

Apart from the growing independence of secondary students one has to question why there is often an apparent fall-off of parental interest in the secondary phase and what might or should be done about it. The involvement of parents varied with catchment area but not all middle-class catchments, as one might expect, had an active parent voice, though on balance they are more likely to do so.

The answer seems to lie in how willing schools are, in fact, to involve parents and how far they find this contact possible to manage constructively. Under the competitive conditions of open enrolment we have been prepared as professionals to market to parents and to package all manner of information for them, but on the whole, despite the Government's emphasis on customers, a residual distrust of parents' capacity to discern or to moderate their unquenchable demands often has heads and governors holding them off like Michael Caine in *Zulu*. Schools are more accessible these days and more friendly but on the deeper issues of educational policy and organization there is still a tendency for professionals to defend their corner.

Joan Sallis has, of course, been fighting this attitude for years and cites in her book, *Schools, Parents and Governors* (1988, p 63), the hostility she met from teachers generally at the suggestion that they should share more with parents. She recognized perhaps earlier than most that 'the defensive teacher is the worst enemy of a better resourced and respected service, which can never ... be achieved without massive united pressure by all those, who use, work in and value the public education system'.

We may have moved a long way from the days when a school gate might blazon 'NO PARENTS BEYOND THIS POINT', but despite all manner of protestations on the part of heads to parents that they are welcome to register their concerns, and even to visit during the school day, many are too shy to take this up. The authority patterns of yesteryear are not so easily shaken off and many parents are still very uncomfortable in schools which as institutions seem to have their own esoteric laws. There is a feeling of being hurried and harried often by the size and potential impersonality of big secondary establishments where their youngsters seem to disappear from view, swallowed by the complex machine. This is not helped, of course, by the conventional type of parents' evenings where parents often have to stand in queues to see the subject teacher with little privacy, and where teachers are conditioned to see parental contact as a chore rather than an opportunity.

Media influence on parents

It is not surprising, therefore, that schools remain remote and mysterious places to many parents and that they become susceptible to the glib and simplistic representations of schools in the media, where there is often a lack of sophisticated voice in the exercise of analysis and arguments for what might be occurring in society and in our schools. A 'tabloid press knee-jerk' parental reaction was cited by one of the heads interviewed who despaired at the superficiality of so many parental concerns. If this is the case then it is certainly exacerbated and fostered by the sloganizing and packaging of complex educational issues in the popular press, exemplified in a critique in the *Times Educational Supplement* on the treatment of GMS:

> *Sun* bangs hard on the opt out drum ... Mums and Dads were called on to sign up and in that ever helpful 10-things-you-need-to-know *Sun* style, the paper detailed how to put the Tories' keynote education policy into action ... It was left to the journalists from rival newspapers in reports from the teacher trade unions' conferences to point out this week 10 things *Sun* readers needed to know about opting out, but weren't told ...(1 May 1992).

The *TES* then goes on to highlight through quotes from these papers some of the complexities ignored. Clearly, we are all as good at decision-making as the information we are given or seek out. The possibilities in a free press for distortion and misinformation are tremendous.

Alasdair MacIntyre in *The Idea of an Educated Public* (1987, p 19) is very pessimistic about an improvement in this situation because society today lacks an interpretative tradition in relation to concepts and values:

> An educated community can exist only where there is some large degree of shared background beliefs and attitudes, informed by the widespread reading of a common body of texts, texts which are accorded canonical status within that particular community ... So not every literate and reading public is an educated public; mass literacy in a society which lacks both canonical texts and a tradition in interpretative understanding is more likely to produce a condition of public mindlessness than an educated public.

If this is indeed the case, and I believe it is, then there is all the more reason for schools to see the mutual education of schools and their public as a considerable priority. Instead of suppressing the potential for value conflict, heads and governors must learn to bring it into the open for general examination and sometimes allow their communities to resolve these differences themselves through a process of mutual education.

School communities and mutual education

In their more autonomous position as both 'businesses' and centres of education and community values, schools should be endeavouring to manage all manner of concerns, through enabling that community to exercise mutual education. The professionals have a role in giving their advice and, if they feel it necessary, yes, their bottom line, but the community also has a role in redefining the common purposes of the school and in building up in partnership with professionals an evolving tradition of interpretative understanding. Schools must seek to build communities whose members can relate to the school and to each other.

It is not always a matter of responding only but of including parents in discussing the dilemmas and complexities. The benefit of such a stance was exemplified in the knowledge displayed by one chair of governors about the reading of examination league tables:

> CHAIR: Regarding exam results, we have a full report given to the governing body of each pupil who sat their exams, of what they were expected to get, what they thought they would get, and what they ended up with. That gives you a very different knowledge of how your exams have gone. There is no way now that I would walk into a school and ask how many A's, how many B's did you get, because it means nothing, because you don't know the sort of pupil they have there at that time.

This governor was able, as a local parent, to carry her knowledge out into the local community and to argue from a position of clear information, and this she evidently did. It is understanding how things work that builds trust, not any bamboozling. Locally there is more chance to deal with the dialogue and this schools must learn to do.

Activist parents are always surprised at the apparent apathy of other parents. They, themselves, have not found schools daunting and they cannot imagine why others should. I asked one chair how he had tried to combat the apparent apathy:

> CHAIR: To be honest it is mainly ... supporting the staff, and making the staff aware of the fact that we are aware of the problem ...
> SW: But you haven't come up with any particular mechanisms that you would actively set up, for example parent surgeries, getting the

parents in to talk to the governors? How does your annual meeting go?

CHAIR: Sadly it is a disaster. If we get three people we're lucky.

SW: Have you talked of ways in which you could try to engage them?

CHAIR: We are constantly doing things, and we try to get ourselves in the press as much as possible, advertising what we are doing and why we are doing it.

This was the school which was facing a falling roll, where the head was agonizing on how far he wished to ₃o in compromising the school's values. However, no controversy had as yet got beyond the school's walls: the anguish was mainly being worked out within. But the bonding of human beings does not come from the peddling of positive images only and the rhetoric of value statements, it comes from people living out the complexities together. In its concern over not bringing back uniform the school might consider how to make this value point a real plus in its projection of the school. It might consider involving the students and through them their parents in a real debate of the issue. If the students were seen to be articulate and sensible by other parents, in such a bold move they could prove to be convincing advocates for the very policy that the school holds dear.

It is true that such a strategy might contain risks, but internal agonizing does not move the matter forward either. If the school could trust its parents and students on this point then perhaps the perceived apathy would also begin to diminish. If schools are serious about parental involvement, and here is the nub of it, then trusting relationships have to be built up: sharing value-questions with parents has a strong bonding effect, even if there is not total agreement. Heads and governors need to develop such competence in managing voice and relationships if parents are not simply to vote with their feet.

The bonding factor

Sometimes the opportunities for voice pop up in informal situations and these must be grasped. For example in my own College I was in the middle of a talk to our 'Village Society' who had asked me to speak on the history of the College. As we have the only public Bauhaus building in this country designed by Walter Gropius and Maxwell Fry, I was commenting on the philosophy of the Bauhaus which was to see technology as subservient to the human spirit: a tool, as it were. A parent in the audience suddenly responded to this with an exasperated exclamation that he had always suspected in our apparent Arts bias that we downgraded Science as a subject. The audience, who had evidently not read my comments that way, protested but his feeling was so strong that I asked him in for a coffee and went through our curriculum rationale and time allocation.

Science was demonstrated to have ample time and status and I explained that the Arts, which he saw as a total waste of time, figured in the National Curriculum; at that time, too, they were not envisaged as optional post-14. He begged to differ in seeing them as an important component but went away reasonably mollified. At the next annual parents' evening for governors, someone asked if we had thought of having governors' surgeries, and 'my' parent spoke up warmly that there was no need for that as anyone could approach the head if they wanted to. He chuckled that he and I had not necessarily agreed over everything but that I would listen. Whatever the state of the Arts and Sciences, I had made a friend who respected my views, perhaps because I had taken his seriously. Indeed, when the family had to move away because of his job, he came to see me and explain. He thanked me for all the school had done and still persisted in his hobby-horse about the place of Science, but it was a friendly and tolerant conversation.

This small incident demonstrated to me, if I had not been aware of it already, that we should not be afraid of a conflict of voice. It is, in fact, this fear of the potency of individual voice to some extent which has perhaps led us into the market forces mechanism in the first place. It is felt that if people are allowed voice then weaker voices are not heard. The market, however, has its own iniquities, too, and these can only be combated by enabling voice, however dangerous that situation may be. It is safer to rely on persuasion than the silent iniquity of market forces alone and thus there is a need for parental voice to come through to be listened to and in some instances to be argued with. What may at least happen in that discussion is that relationships and bonding may occur, which certainly do not occur in the silences of mechanisms such as the market place.

Sometimes, too, parents modify each other. This happens frequently at the Parents–Staff Association and did recently over the issue of parents making voluntary contributions. One parent wanted us to levy a contribution each year and another saw this as compounding the inequalities which already exist in the state system. We did in the end decide to invite parental donations on a voluntary basis to be used in cases of need such as costs in visiting universities and so on. It is much more potent sometimes when parents counter arguments because it relieves the critical parent of the paranoid assumption that some authority figure is denying them their right. It also takes the heat off the professionals who can be part of the discussion without finding themselves in the 'Aunt Sally' position.

For example, an interesting difference of viewpoint arose when at one and the same time I was tackled over our Record of Achievement. One parent wanted normative assessment with some sort of league table on his daughter's performance in the class, year and possibly universe, while another parent of a dyslexic child begged me to redesign a section so that her son would get more positive comments. She loved the 'can-do' emphasis. I made the mental note to run a parents' session on the reports in the next academic year and would make a point of getting both sets of parents there and would possibly review our internal formats in the light of the discussion. Such discussion would not cause a head necessarily to abandon what s/he saw as professional sense but if some shifts were possible a sensible head would not wish to stand out against them for no good reason.

Appropriate styles of contact

Not all schools, however, will find parents coming in to contribute or challenge in this way. This difficulty comes through very clearly in schools in poorer areas such as inner cities – the very schools which John Major is now challenging heads and governors to improve through the threat of closure or management 'hit squads'. If parents are to become more involved in such areas, different sorts of contact and information may be needed. What came through in the survey was that parents in all schools would turn out for reports consultation evenings; it was the committee-type organization that parents in more working-class areas eschewed. One of the heads confirmed this pattern very clearly:

> We have only got one parent governor, we can't get any more however hard we try. Annual parents' meetings have collapsed and virtually disappeared without trace. The various formal committee

structures that involve parents hardly ever work. And yet 85 per cent of our parents visit once per year minimum to receive their child's report ... And what all that says to me is, that formal committee structures, formal methods of consultation and formal participation of the stakeholders are a very professional middle-class construct ... people find forms of expression of these things in different ways, and our job as a college is on the one hand not to be patronizing about that, but on the other hand is to find out what those different ways are and to enable them.

The difficulty becomes compounded if professionals begin to accept this pattern as inevitable and parents continue not to challenge the organization. Though in all the pressing business of schools it is tempting to take an apparently quiescent catchment area for granted, in the present volatile situation it is certainly not prudent or educationally justifiable. If schools, and certainly community schools and colleges, are educative centres then they should be such for all associated with them.

Community schools have access to the community through other channels than the school formal function and should take advantage of this contact whenever possible. For example, the school cited above is a community college, and despite parental resistance to school functions and committees, there is a well-attended community programme which creates a sense of belonging to, and familiarity with, the institution. In non-designated community schools, however, opportunities can be created to make the institution more parent-friendly: school productions involving the students and curriculum evenings where the children are demonstrating their learning and taking charge of their parents can help. Schools are also investing in celebratory newsletters beyond the glossy prospectus to give real insight in a professional and attractive format to the workings of the school. Such publications need to reflect the real life of the school and involve the achievements of a wide variety of children. The format, too, needs to be lively and attractive and thus worth reading.

Indeed, rather than selling an image which may in the end be off-putting to many parents if it is too formal and pretentious, the prospectus and newsletter can set a tone and create a window on the school with immediacy. One chairperson who was a marketing consultant set great store by such impressions and information:

Because of my marketing background I have been heavily involved with [the college newspaper], the prospectus, and so on. To me prospective parents, which are the lifeblood of any school, take an awful lot from the prospectus. If it is a drab, dreary, 50-page document which talks of the colour of shoes and standards of dress and nothing else, then it doesn't convey the school ... it should tell the reader about [the school] in total, not about different segments, different rules, and so on.

The newspaper and prospectus were up to date and, yes, perhaps quite slick, but the difference was that they were celebrating the whole and not glib value-packages such as one sees where prospectuses have pretentious views of school façades or computers in every photograph. There is image-making and there is access to the heart of establishments which good marketing can bring.

The same was true of the school where the head had been successful in combating a falling roll. All his contact with parents was personalized through individual appointments and surgeries, through open days while the school was in action and through a weekly newsletter which celebrated individual children's achievements in all fields. The personal approach to parents and children seems to be more important in those communities which may be put off by formality and façades designed to hype up the respectability of the school and its sobriety. Heads and governors need to consider their approaches carefully but should not assume that parents are apathetic or that easily taken in. In most respects humanity and warmth are strong attractions to parents entrusting their child to the school.

The style of contact may have to be different in different circumstances and, though success in involving parents cannot be guaranteed in all instances, a more strategic focus on this area needs the will and lateral thinking of heads, particularly as the Government has now made this a performance indicator for successful schools. The indication of that will was demonstrated in the case of two schools mentioned: the one had invested in a public relations person and good communications and the other, with the expertise of a motivated chair of governors, in good quality prospectuses and newspaper.

The personal factor

The major factor in all instances is, of course, a welcoming atmosphere and the feeling of being taken seriously. It is important that any outreach work does not attempt to patronize, but giving up on parental involvement, either because it is too intrusive or apparently apathetic, is defeatist. New strategies have to be considered and the most effective do appear to be those which give parents and pupils *personalized* time. This is not necessarily personal time but refers to the quality of the contact and the environment in which that contact occurs.

In the case of the City Technology College visited in the survey, for example, the children are not simply allocated by the authority and there is, therefore, an admittedly time-consuming process where each child is interviewed at the school. While schools like my own have personalized induction considerably over the years, including, in our case, the personal profile which youngsters prepare and bring with them as a talking point with their tutor, a personal interview with parents and child would clearly punctuate induction more meaningfully. It is a strategy worth considering and could be divided in my own College among the tutors who, in our vertical House system, have six new pupils each year. This would be a further refinement of the fairly personal approach we have to parents and students already through Primary Induction and the New Parents Evening where, after being greeted by me, the parents and students meet with House heads and tutors prior to further contact in the September.

However more personalized contact is achieved, it seems to me important that schools do not simply see their intakes as a list of children or a whole group; some personalizing of admissions needs to be worked on as it has to be in the private, CTC or GMS sectors. It is doubtful, however, that it should reach the point described by an independent school head where he was continually rung at home about often quite trivial matters. He humorously described juggling dinner for his children with the late arrival home of his wife and an interminable telephone conversation with a parent over bonfire smoke. However, though long-suffering on occasions, he recognized that this was a service parents felt they paid for.

Parent consultation evenings need in some way to be rethought also into more staggered formats where interviews are professional consultations rather than queues and cattle markets. Schools have tried to rethink these over the years and are increasingly bringing in more informative reports and, in some cases, an initial tutor-based consultation in the younger years at least which can be followed up with subject consultations. Headteachers do need to find ways within the 1265 hours of directed time to make these consultations parent and pupil friendly, with interviews with students and their parents spread out over the school year. It is a logistics problem that needs to be addressed and is one that is helped by reports whose formats and process are integral to teaching and learning. In this way they can be formative for the student's learning and self-awareness as well as informative for parents.

Often the questions which parents raise at consultation evenings could be addressed in an open session with groups of parents or user-friendly handbooks, so that the actual consultation interview focuses on progress. In more deprived areas, where parental attendance can be low for committee work, parents nevertheless seem to turn out for consultation evenings: the quality of these interviews becomes an important feature in encouraging further contact with the school and possibly getting school values across.

The need for boundaries

At the same time as schools are encouraging contact of all kinds, from curriculum talks to progress reports, there must be an understanding set out by the school on some boundaries to protect the energies and professional position of staff. In a customer-driven culture it must be the job of the head to ensure that both parents and teachers are given due respect and consideration. Any head or teacher who has turned up in all good heart for a social function of the Parent–Staff Association only to be collared by a parent over some desperate detail of their youngster's day will know the weariness of the busman's holiday.

Though the formality of committee structures may not be appropriate in all areas, too much informality of individual contact also needs to be avoided. Teachers may find themselves rung up rather like the private school head who saw it as part of his function. Though sometimes such contact may be necessary, it is important that the friendliness demonstrated by schoolteachers is not abused. If clear complaint channels and sympathetic contact arrangements are built in, then I believe parents will use these more and more considerately. Complaints procedures and contact points need clear school's publicity, and opportunities to explain these procedures should be taken at admission time. The school secretaries must also be trained in good interface with the public and we have added to that at Impington a

'Front of House' system where an office is staffed throughout the day to troubleshoot with confidence crises that arise: agitated parents, informal and impromptu visits. If access is rhetorical rather than real then the distrust of parents will grow; the better the first contact with the school can be then the less likely it is that any subsequent contact will carry distrust. Furthermore, that message is carried by word of mouth to others.

The fact is that parents and teachers do have a lot to share with each other over individual children and most schools in the sample had excellent information systems. However, these often fell short of real parental say and voice. Parents, working initially it is true from an interest in their own child, can be encouraged to share in more general ideas about the aims and values of the curriculum and the funding of that curriculum. What is at stake is not the desirability of this but an appropriate and manageable way of doing it which puts parents at their ease and ensures that teachers' energies are not exploited.

It is important, too, that the parents understand the boundaries in which the schools work and how far, within resources and legislative guidelines, they can manoeuvre. It was interesting, for example, in one school's consultation evening with parents over GMS in Cambridgeshire, that parents were not aware that that school had been working with a devolved budget for many years; indeed, Cambridgeshire has played a major part since 1983 in piloting devolved funding, leading to Local Management of Schools (LMS) and now to GMS. Given this history, it was significant that parents were still not aware of this important move and thought that with GMS the governors and head would be propelled into a daunting cut and thrust of business ethics for which they were wholly unprepared.

Parent power

There has been a marked increase in parent power in recent years, with parent associations and individuals lobbying local and national politicians on all manner of issues, from underfunding to school closures. The reforms to date have mostly beleaguered the profession more than the public at large. Clearly as the GMS wave and the issues associated with it grow, more and more students and parents are going to be affected. Parental concern and involvement are bound to hot up and it is recognized already by various pressure and interested groups that a stronger parental voice is needed, particularly to represent those parents who, for whatever reason, find it difficult to engage themselves in it. The *Times Educational Supplement* reported on this:

> A powerful collection of parental pressure groups has come together with the aim of forming a single voice which carries more political clout. In an exploratory meeting funded by the Paul Hamlyn Foundation, groups including the Advisory Centre for Education and the National Confederation of Parent–Teacher associations discussed the possibility of setting up a campaigning body based around a national magazine for parents (29 May 1992).

However, though such voice is important it is no substitute for understanding and an empowerment at the local level. If customers are to become truly discerning, as the White Paper assumes them to be, then they need to understand how schools work and to feel that they have some say in that. Schools, therefore, have an educative role to play in trying to undo glib assumptions about schools and to close the gap which exists between 'them and us'. Education must be two-way; it must be mutual education. Relationships of mutual benefit to parents and schools need to be built up if we are to create traditions of interpretative understanding (MacIntyre, 1987) then there must be an effort to overcome parental reticence. Education is an exciting business and schools can and need to convey that message by bringing parents closer to the experiences of their children through their children. I cite Peter Abbs (1979, p 119):

> If we define education as expressive activity, as the continuous process through which we give shape to life itself, then the educational institutions must in turn be seen as clay to be shaped according to the evolving conceptions of all its members. If individuality and community are complementary concepts, then we cannot have a full education for the child until we have secured a sense of true community in our schools.

Chapter 5

The Sharing of Dilemmas

Shared silence or voice?

It is clear that Government reforms for education place great store on
the discipline of Hirschman's notion of exit. In their concern to effect
speedy remedial change, the Government sees in such discipline a
responsive mechanism which is likely to overcome the inertia of
traditionally slow-moving institutions. Voice as a change agent, on the
other hand, is more cumulative and diffuse in its effectiveness, as
Hirschman goes on to explain (1970, p 16):

> In all these respects, voice is just the opposite of exit. It is a far more
> 'messy' concept because it can be graduated, all the way from faint
> grumbling to violent protest; it implies articulation of one's critical
> opinions rather than a private, 'secret' vote in the anonymity of a
> supermarket; and finally, it is direct and straightforward rather than
> roundabout. Voice is political action par excellence.

Advocates of the market, Hirschman continues, think that their
mechanism is more efficient, and he cites Milton Friedman, whose
belief in a voucher system for education rests on the efficacy of exit.
Without the free market, Friedman maintains (1955, p 129), parents
can only exert their views of education by moving house to get into the
catchment area of the favoured school. 'For the rest,' writes Friedman,
'[parents] can express their views only through cumbrous political
channels.' Cumbrous though such channels may be, Hirschman (1970,
p 17) believes they are the only channels with which we as a society can
work:

In the first place, Friedman considers withdrawal or exit as the 'direct' way of expressing one's unfavourable views of an organization. A person less well trained in economics might naively suggest that the direct way of expressing views is to express them! Secondly, the decision to voice one's views and efforts to make them prevail are contemptuously referred to by Friedman as a resort to 'cumbrous political channels'. But what else is the political, and indeed the democratic, process than the digging, the use, and hopefully the slow improvement of these very channels?

It is between these arguments that the management of schools now falls: school managers can either succumb to accepting exit as the dominant determining factor in their decisions and will to exert influence, or they can accept the messiness of voice and see it as the function of their institutions to foster that voice in any way they can. In many ways it is not entirely a matter of choice, for the very tensions which exit engenders will perforce bring out voice, albeit, again, in a cumulative and ad hoc fashion. It is perhaps a fact of life in any democracy that voice remains inert precisely because any redress of dissatisfaction requires an effort that most of us would prefer not to have to make. It is not a question of apathy only, but in life's general pressures it is one of keeping our powder dry for the major battles we face in the ordinary business of living and working. People in general only tend to erupt into protest when some destabilizing factor directly and immediately affects them. Thus, if at the same time as it offers exit the market also offers considerable disruption, then the normal torpor of human affairs is likely to be replaced by more active voice.

In fact, the processes being used in the reforms to contrive a market for schools are those which require some degree of voice and parental decision. Though professionals and local government are no longer deciding the shape of education in terms of types of schools, and they are no longer the dominant force in designing the curriculum, they are having to advise parents and governors on decisions which they, in their part in the popular control of schools, have to make. This is inevitably a political education and it is an encouragement of qualitative thinking and voice.

Despite, therefore, market conditions where silent exit could prevail, a potentially participative process is underway; voice is becoming more prevalent. Matters like ballots on GMS have woken some communities to attend to education more fully than otherwise would have been the case. The fact of the parental vote and the implications of its freedoms have affected parents and governors in a variety of ways. Education has never been higher on the public agenda, and the progress of the changes is caught in the media gaze as mini and maxi conflicts and crises emerge.

Voice in the media

Sometimes, indeed, the media are called upon to expose a difference of view which has erupted into aggressive voice rather than faint grumbling. Perhaps a typical example was the reported case of a GMS school allegedly 'getting rid of troublesome boys':

> A Tory council has called for an investigation that an opted out school is weeding out low-achieving children and trouble-makers ... the Tory chairman of the education committee said that between 13 and 15 pupils have been withdrawn or excluded from the school this year. 'It seems something very wrong is going on there. I am not against schools opting out, but I want to cut out this question of them selecting pupils in this way.' A Labour councillor ... said: 'My fear is the creation of sin-bin schools. If the authority had been in control the inspectors would have gone in by now' (*Independent* 26 July 1992).

I do not wish to judge the situation above on the basis of a newspaper report, but the dilemma is an interesting one, illustrative of the new culture. The rules on exclusions are not likely to be different for an opted out school; but support and advice to parents could be lacking. Parents can always contest an exclusion and appeal to the governing body. However, the LEA has been there in the past to advise governors of legal risks and to advise parents also of their rights. Parents have not had to fight such battles on their own before and schools will have been more constrained by the paternal LEA. Indeed acting as ombudsman for parents may well become a central part of the work of LEAs in whatever form they remain.

Given the possible legal implications of such action, however, it will not be long before the more astute parents do learn their rights and, as similar issues become more and more public, there will be a change in how parents receive and react to such matters. The parents in this case felt they had not been advised of their rights, as the same article indicates:

> Parents of former pupils say they were not made aware of their rights when they agreed to withdraw their children. The governing body is legally required to approve suspensions or expulsions, and parents have a right of appeal. Expulsions from state schools are rare, and usually applied only for highly disruptive behaviour.

The fact is that where parents find themselves in a situation where they have to shift for themselves in the freedoms of the market place, that same freedom which sharpens up practice through the threat of exit can also sharpen up voice for those people for whom the principle of exit has not worked. Of course, not all parents will be as able as others to represent themselves: the market assumes great capability and discernment – the perfectly equipped customer, in fact. Children, however, *are* dependent, and if the market fails them, they will have lost their one opportunity for a good education – the very thing which the White Paper of 1992 was pledged to avoid. The safeguarding of such children makes the education and empowerment of a public a pressing matter.

The education of a public

In the absence of any legitimated authority, however, to undertake such a function, who assumes the leadership role in educating a public? The increasing involvement of the public in the dilemmas of educational change today puts the good of all children in the hands of parents, whether all parents are up to the task or not. Thus the schools are facing both a more assertive public and in some instances a more dependent one. The professional role of schools has to take account of both possibilities.

A school can either embrace openness and anticipate a more informed public, and indeed contribute to that public's education, or it can be tempted into a more cynical and patronizing role in manipulating that public, if it can, according to its own agenda. This might involve the school in rhetoric about standards to justify exclusion or selection, or it might involve the façades described in a previous chapter. All schools will combine elements of this because the market invites such posturing and compromise – all is fair in love, war and the market place ...

However, a social institution such as a school should at least be trying to live up to nobler aims, and one safeguard is to practise as far as possible an open examination of values within the establishment and outside it. Manipulation may win some battles but it will not win the war – the war between the worst and best in our social selves. Adopting a cynical approach, apart from being morally suspect, may not, in any case, attract much loyalty in the long run, for the school's relationships will not be based on voice and relationship but on a take-it-or-leave-it situation – exit.

If schools are to maintain quality and integrity as socially responsible institutions, then the responsibilities devolved to them must not be to take advantage of the more vulnerable parent and child, but to act with even more integrity because of the very danger of moral compromise. No school is of course perfect or operates in a perfect world, but the option of exit is inevitably a self-interested answer, and quite possibly a very selfish answer.

Only open examination of dilemmas can resolve unfortunate corruptions and pave the way to the best integrity possible in any given situation. It is better for heads and governors to honour professional and legal guidelines than face the possibility of a manipulated public finding them wanting. For the sake of prudence, therefore, rather than even moral integrity, heads and governors ignore such reasonableness at the risk of a woken public recognizing cynicism for what it is and acquiring the skills to challenge it.

Thus, the enlightenment of the public to the intricacies of the present state of education which current debates are fostering can either have something of the *fait accompli* about it as governors and heads try to dictate or manipulate their own terms, or it can have the beginnings of trust and shared concerns. If schools are prepared to treat people and children well and fairly, and if they are prepared to see the public as basically interested and well-meaning rather than wholly cynical, gullible or of no real account, then the rewards of loyalty which can ensue from the mingling of voices would seem a greater prize than the benefits of manipulative processes and the avoidance of voice.

The public consultations over GMS are opening up a questioning mode of 'why' rather than simply 'how' which can pave the way for many other 'why'-questions. This opportunity for greater public consciousness and debate is one that should be grasped, for it serves as an opening to a number of dilemmas which communities should be sharing with schools, not least because it is so much more interesting and rewarding to work *with* a community than purely *on its behalf*. Not to try to do so perpetuates an authoritarianism or paternalism inappropriate to the public's schools. Treating people in this positive way is also an insurance that the public does not submit to authoritarianism and paternalism in other parts of their life: the best safeguard for us all.

The grown-up culture

The release from local authority control denotes a very 'grown-up' culture where no other 'parent' professional is around to hold the head's or governors' hands. Of course, LMS has been moving in this direction already, and certainly in Cambridgeshire the step to GMS is not necessarily such a great one, for schools already have considerable freedom to decide whether they buy local authority services or whether they shop around for other bargains. As the managers and policy-makers of increasingly independent entities, school heads and governors are finding themselves in the front line with the public over all sorts of issues and values. The new autonomy of schools, which the market forces philosophy seeks to foster, puts schools into both an exhilarating and lonely position.

In this new 'freedom' heads and governors may seize opportunities and flexibilities to be innovative and creative; they are also at liberty to be criticized for those innovations or for any mistakes that they might be judged to have made. Hence the reported criticism by parents of primary school governors in the sleepy village of Crowland, Lincolnshire. The parents objected to the decision of the governors not to employ an extra teacher and to hold the money back. The decision to retain some monies may have related to the anticipation of eventualities which the governors deemed to be important. However, through perhaps a failure of communication, the parents failed to appreciate the reasons for the decision and passed a vote of no confidence in the governing body of that school (*Observer* 26 April 1992).

The media, too, have increasingly an influence on the public's perception of educational issues and dilemmas. In the case of Special Needs, for example, Radio Cambridgeshire, June 1992, reported that parents were finding it difficult to get their children's needs met under the terms of the 1981 Act. There have also been reported fears, as I mentioned earlier, that some local children may not get or keep places in their local GMS school where heads will want to demonstrate good examination results and good discipline; this concern applies not least to cases of Special Needs, particularly in the cases of disruptive children. This together with national coverage of the problem is focusing the public and politicians on the questions that need to be addressed.

This greater openness about difficult issues should be welcomed, for it is only in this way that the public, on whose discernment and skills informed choice in a free economy depends, will be able to help itself. Media coverage can be very variable but it does at its best create a situation where the worst aspects of alleged self-interest can be examined. There are unfortunately no perfect safeguards in a free press against simplistic attitudes and this is where the openness of schools can temper the situation: schools must bring the community closer to the school processes, closer to the children themselves – but I will come back to this point.

Lest we feel that the task of educating a public is too great in this fragmented customer-culture today, it is important to remember that there have not been perfect safeguards in the past: LEAs have varied in quality and effectiveness just as much as individual schools. However, the demise of LEAs puts more onus on schools to communicate and consult with parents and other schools as effectively and constructively as possible. Greater information and debate in an age of mass communications systems will inevitably involve the media as well as other channels and school heads and governors will inevitably be asked, as now, for their views and comments. School leaders are already very used to such interest from local papers but perhaps, beyond highlighting great achievements, not all are used to being part of informative programmes and debate.

The use of media will become more significant in communicating to a public and such journalism at its best does a great deal to assist the complex debate: heads, in particular, will need greater skills in the use of the media to engender understanding and debate and, provided they concern themselves with the effects of any changes on the well-being of children rather than political propaganda, they are not betraying any professional position. Governing bodies, on the other hand, are now the political voice of the school and may well find themselves playing an increasing part as political spokespersons in the press; skills in handling the media become therefore an important competence for governors to develop as public debate hots up. Many chairs of governors will have experienced this already as their views are sought after meetings and press statements have to be issued on a variety of questions such as GMS ballots, and so on.

The education of a public is not a one way traffic: professionals may fear meddling from non-professionals but they should also fear indifference or silence. Governors are an important link with the wider community and it is far better, and indeed more exciting, for heads to anticipate that interest in governor voice than to try to drown or ignore it. Where good relationships are built up heads and governors can more easily trust each other and parents with questions or dilemmas and vice versa. The mediation of complex and different values among school stakeholders is always a matter of judgement and may often require boldness, but it is preferable to silence and unexplained decisions. Leadership is essential, of course; confident direction which allows for some voice and modification demonstrates the really open and mature organization. It is also a safeguard, in an increasingly fragmented culture, against the dangers of the few voices rather than many.

Bonding and loyalties

In the present climate of change many school communities are going through very steep learning curves. Though we might well wish to avoid the controversy and anguish which some professionals and parents have experienced in this new situation, we are nevertheless beginning to see communities having to face up to the values of market forces as new opportunities and latent conflicts come to the fore. The rapid pace of the reforms has to date largely beleaguered the profession, but now, as media coverage shows, the wider community is increasingly involved. No governing body would wish to find itself caught up in the problems of one school in the survey which found itself involved in litigation when a thwarted local authority took the Secretary of State for Education to court. However, the experience certainly instilled in that school new insights and a greater sense of identity. The reorganization plans of the authority to reduce surplus places had been negated by the decision to allow a school to go grant-maintained, which contradicted the Secretary's circulars of previous years to take surplus classroom space out for reasons of cost.

The head caught up in the litigation described the experience which, though worrying, he found far from dull:

> I was actually driving my car ... when I heard on the national news that the judge ... had granted a judicial review to [the county] over the school, which meant that the decision to give Grant-Maintained Status was revoked, that the acting head (namely myself) was no longer acting head (although I had already resigned my deputy headship) and that the Secretary of State was asked officially by the courts to reconsider his decision. So then we were in turmoil. I had no right to enter the building except if I was given permission (as I was once or twice). The governing body could not hold meetings in here, we had to go into one of our governors' offices in the city ... We waited and held our breath for five or six weeks until the decision was announced on 30 March by John MacGregor ... he reaffirmed his decision to allow Grant Maintained Status ... Now, that was a fascinating time for me because I spent a lot of time on the telephone with all sorts of people, trying to find out what was going to happen and what the chances were, what I could do. What I learnt about politics and the law and so on, well, I could write a book about it ... It was worrying, but it was absolutely fascinating. It was an incredible experience for me.

Such sharing of dilemmas has a powerful bonding effect upon the protagonists caught up in it. This particular school had chosen to go down the GMS route because the school had been threatened with closure over a long period and the governors and local community found the constant uncertainty and threat untenable. Finally the LEA had indicated that the school would become a Sixth Form College. This further set-back only served to reinforce the local community's determination, as the chair indicated:

> The school is held in particular affection and regard by a wide community within the [area] ... There was a groundswell of

resentment. I think ... parents ... got tired and fed up with it. I think that they said that enough is enough, the grant-maintained possibility became available and ... the governors grasped that with, I think, the support of the parents, with open arms.

Such stories of particular histories and allegiances reflect that the Government's plan to encourage different types of school hits a real nerve. Communities can be loyal to their schools; they feel they do belong to them and, though the market system is fraught with problems, there is generally resistance to return to the paternalistic model of LEAs and notions of rationalization in the interests of economy or anything else.

The signs in the White Paper 1992 are that GMS will not necessarily be the escape route it was for the school above, for there is in the Paper a declared intention to reduce surplus places identified by the Audit Commission, and this inevitably means more school closures. However, communities are still likely to put up a fight and in sharing the vicissitudes of such situations, not only are professionals and non-professionals drawn closer together, but communities gain in self-reliance which would otherwise not have been the case. The breaking up of the empire, then, and the sharing of the dilemmas which go with that in many cases, is creating a new stratum of people who are gaining confidence, know-how and insight: all this constitutes the education of a public.

For all schools, however, the engaging of people in the real dilemmas and issues facing the school cannot be underestimated. More than this, schools will need these allies in their new state, for indeed no school is an island and cannot afford to be so. Engaging stakeholders is not only an educative matter, a matter of voices rather than voice, but it is also an important factor in bonding and loyalty which is not otherwise available, as Hirschman emphasizes, in an exit market-culture. In the pluralism and silences of today's culture it is only too easy for our society either to sink into no voice, fragmented voices or the domination of very few voices. Thus, it is the educative function and, indeed, duty of the thinking school to encourage and cultivate *voices*.

The problem of few voices

A political orthodoxy is colouring increasingly the make-up of committees concerned with the curriculum, as *Times Educational Supplement* reporter Geraldine Hackett (17 July 1992) comments:

> For the past couple of years Education Secretaries have been appointing people thought to have views in line with Government policy and John Patten appears willing to follow the trend.
>
> Much of what was once regarded as right-wing has become the new orthodoxy.

Ted Wragg, Professor of Education at Exeter University, recalls R. A. Butler's warnings about such political intervention:

> [Butler] stated categorically that it was not for ministers to decree the detail of what was taught in schools, and repeated the same message to Churchill when asked what he could do to make children more patriotic. Churchill accepted that politicians should make suggestions rather than try to take control of the curriculum. Far from being good news the packing of key committees responsible for education with politically selected people is utterly alarming (*Sunday Times* 19 July, 1992).

In fact, the reforms for education in this country contrast very much with the improvements to education brought in by Denmark. There, in the 1970s, there was a similar loss of confidence in the system by politicians and an alienation of parents through industrial action on the part of the one teachers' union. As the morale of teachers and parents plummeted, enlightened educationalists in the teachers' professional association came up with new plans and, after pilots in schools and consultation with parents, the Government became sufficiently convinced to adopt the plan as a reform package. The momentum for these reforms was grassroots-generated and, after piloting, endorsed with full party support; an address by a Danish parent and teacher to the RSA on 19 February 1992 (Bach and Christensen, 1992, p 449), explained it thus:

> A huge amount of knowledge from this bottom-up process has been accumulated. The involved schools – teachers, pupils and parents – have experienced the positive feeling of being part of a new project ... It is obvious that schools and teachers working with experiments

have a different spirit ... The Folkeskole – the pupils, the parents, the teachers and the local community – has changed in many ways during the last decade. Today there is a universal aura of respect towards the school and the teachers' work ... The change does not mean there is no criticism from parents, politicians and others about school and teachers but it is the kind of criticism that is given among friends or inside a family.

By contrast, the effect of British reforms is that, though they have been designed to give parents more choice, the nature of that choice is often being decided for them as much as it is being decided for the professionals; however well-meaning, and based on what the Government has discerned parents want, they are nevertheless top-down. They have not involved teachers in any consistent and constructive way and parents, formally, hardly at all. Inevitably, therefore, any real information to parents and consultation with them can now only occur at local level as these reforms are introduced.

It is this corrective factor to an overzealous interest in education which Duncan Graham, former Head of the Curriculum Council envisages. It is precisely because the National Curriculum, despite its flaws, is beginning to provide more quality and coherence for education that so many more parties, including political parties, are wanting more influence in its make-up and content. The safeguard for balance and the integrity of the curriculum, therefore, Duncan Graham sees in greater critical involvement of parents. As the popular determinant of education on so many fronts today, parents need, he feels, to 'own' the curriculum lest it be monopolized:

Everyone needs to share in setting standards and in quality assurance. By destroying the old institutions without putting better in their place, the Government has created a black hole which, if left unfilled, will ensure that none of us will know whether standards are rising or whether the National Curriculum is working.

The National Curriculum is good news. For the first time we have a broadly acceptable indication of entitlement, of targets, of benchmarks and of standards ... We need to protect it from those who fear its success, and from those who recognize a good thing when they see it and want to make it *their* curriculum rather than the nation's (*Observer*, Schools Report, 6 September 1992).

Thus, while there is no possibility in the short term of creating the

Danish bottom-up process from scratch in this country, schools can recognize that they have an educative role to play in opening up school practice, including that now being required of schools under the National Curriculum, to parents – not in any defensive way, but in a truly consultative way. It will only be in opening to parents the dilemmas of the school's practice at close quarters that informed public opinion may start to shape education in England and Wales as it has done in such countries as Denmark. As time goes by there will be inevitable changes and modifications and the more voices involved in that shaping the better.

Opportunity not threat

It is true that the schools feel overloaded and therefore do not relish what might be perceived as extra work, but at the same time the process of GMS ballots and the National Curriculum and all the other outcomes associated with the reforms have to be worked out at school level. This should and must be seen as an opportunity rather than a threat, for it is only in sharing these changes that schools will have the understanding and support of parents, be that in relation to organiza- tional or financial issues or to matters to do with the school curriculum and ethos. During the summer of 1991 the *Cambridge Evening News* emphasized just this point in relation to a budgetary crisis with the headline, 'GIVE US THE FACTS SO WE CAN HELP OUR SCHOOLS' and went on to say:

> It is up to the schools themselves to decide just how much, or how little, of the detail of their budgets they should give to parents. We hope they will reveal all. Not so much to be accountable – although that is a worthy aim in itself – but to explain, to encourage and to seek assistance ...
>
> The more we know, the more we shall understand. Then we shall be able to play our full part in ensuring that our children get the best possible start in life.

Of course, it would be easy to be cynical about the likelihood of parents really bothering to be interested; it would also not be surprising if some heads and governors foresaw and feared the narrow- mindedness of certain parents who would see some spending or curricular organization as extravagant or unnecessary. Nevertheless, the point has to be made that either schools facilitate mutual education within their communities or they will have it done for them. What constitutes an effective school needs more open discussion than it is at present getting; if parents are victims of glib ideas and slogans put out by either politicians or the media, or indeed by the schools themselves, then schools and the profession generally must take some responsibility for that ignorance.

School leaders, and the profession as a whole, need to help the public to stop looking at education through the wrong end of a telescope and that means that some reasonable critique must be made possible within school communities through a sharing of questions and dilemmas. Strong voice is desirable but there need to be some safeguards against too much certainty and conviction of any one voice by allowing voices to come through at all levels of the organization. Schools need to go beyond packaging and marketing to a more educative function: in this way parents can gain real insight into the whys and wherefores of what is taught and how schools are run. There is a need to balance the threat of silent exit with sharing problems, which leads to empowerment, warmth and the safeguard of voices rather than voice.

Chapter 6

Governors as Developers of Policy

Recruitment of governors

The White Paper 1992 made clear reference to governing bodies in terms of 'Quality Assurance' in relation to both LMS and GMS schools. For the most part the Paper focuses on heads, parents and pupils but the governing body is seen to have a major role, with the head, in guarding the school against failure and ensuring improvement. In the case of both failure and improvement, it is nevertheless the governing body which is invoked as having the major duty:

> Schools must not be allowed to fail their pupils. That requires clear and effective action by governing bodies ... the onus for improving schools rests in the first instance on governing bodies and their headteachers. Under the Education (Schools) Act 1992, it will be for governing bodies to draw up and publish an action plan following an inspection report (p 49).

It is recognized, too, that 'an intransigent or divided governing body' (p 21) could put schools at risk and in the case of GMS and LEA schools, the Paper talks of stronger intervention by the Secretary of State (p 21) or LEAs (p 49).

It is, therefore, naturally the case that the recruitment and quality of governors and the working of the governing body are critical factors in how effectively schools are supported in the situation of education today. Yet selection of governors to date has not been rigorous in its expectations of knowledge or training. Nor has sufficient attention been paid to the management of governing bodies as a key team within the school. Anyone can be put forward or come forward as a governor and, indeed, with the greater onus which is now placed on governors' shoulders, there is understandable concern about the suitability and calibre of the people who might stand and the capacity of any governing body to work cohesively and with due confidence about their remit and powers.

In the past, most governors agreed to stand from a sense of well-meaning interest, only to find in more recent times that they are having to face, with heads, great change in education which involves them in a forest of papers and such serious business as budget cuts, teacher redundancies and the complexity of whether or not to seek grant-maintained status. Some obviously view the increased responsibility with eager interest, while others find it onerous and worrying, and not what they expected of a voluntary commitment. Some governors feel they have every right and the expertise to comment on the school curriculum and general organization, while others are embarrassed and daunted at presuming to share a platform with professionals on a wide range of issues.

Management and governance

If schools are to develop as strong institutions providing real entitlement and quality, then a good team of governors is essential. A strong school will be made up of various elements of which the governing body is a vital backbone and backstop. Such strength will only emerge if there is a clear understanding by governors and heads of the difference between *management* and *governance*.

In the pace of change today it has proved difficult for some heads and governors to tease out the parameters of their roles, but it is essential that they do so if the governors and head are to exercise their respective responsibilities effectively. It is perhaps the case that some heads lean too heavily upon governors, particularly where the school cannot afford a good bursar, in matters of devolved finance; sometimes governors themselves imagine that they have to manage the school directly instead of having an accountability to see that good management obtains. The prospect of such 'remote control' management is naturally daunting, as the nervousness of one governor in the survey illustrates:

> I think people are getting rather scared ... [at taking on] more of [this] kind of responsibility. I think there will be a point where people will not be willing to stand, and I think it is one of the ironies of a system that was set up to increase participation, but it is doing the exact opposite ... I think to tell people that they are now responsible for a budget of two million is enough to make them say, 'Well, I can't take that kind of responsibility, because what would happen if something went wrong?' ... we are lucky, we have ... a deputy borough treasurer ... But what if we didn't have him? I know, having acted as treasurer for [an organization] for three years. It was awful, I mean it really did take up an awful lot of time and I really did worry about it ... So I cannot see that 'ordinary' people are going to be able to do it.

What is significant about this reaction, which reflects the feeling of many governors, is the confusion of management and governance. The governing body is not responsible for managing the budget but for ensuring that all reasonable good management prevails. Confidence in the school's management team is therefore essential, as is an attention to the sort of infrastructure the school needs to manage financial devolvement. Undue pressure on the head or the governors is the issue behind the governor's anxiety and thus ways have to be found to combat this. It is a question of getting to grips with a finance policy which will deliver clear information and thus the possibility of strategic planning rather than book-keeping, whether that is closer to governor skills or not.

Similarly, though head and governors would wish to have sight of annotated budget print-outs, it is a waste of governor quality time to spend meetings on financial minutiae. It should be the policy decisions which focus such meetings; the rest is a matter of management. If governors are to see the wood for the trees, the extent of their responsibilities needs to be worked out in relation to governance, not management, and heads should be concerned to pitch information and policy-making accordingly. It is true that many governors feel happier with the minutiae: they may find in such concrete detail a comfort in problem-solving and feeling useful which the uncharted prospect of educational concerns does not immediately engender. No harm is done in capitalizing on such skill provided it does not simply deflect head and governors from real policy issues. The more lost in detail a governing body becomes, the less will their sights be focused on governance as opposed to management.

Apathy or dependency

Of course, such a focus deflects governors also from other issues which the head may well not wish to share. There is no doubt that many heads have preferred a relatively inactive governing body in the past because it has left them free to get on with running the school. The same impatient fear of superficiality sometimes obtains in regard to governing bodies, as it does in regard to parents. Equally, given the increased responsibilities of governors, the voluntary nature of the role and the pressures on professionals mean that it can suit all concerned to encourage able and confident heads to get on and run their schools. Several chairs mentioned that, having considerable faith in their headteachers, they believed in management (that word again) by exception: this is to say that if the head appeared to know what s/he was doing then any intervention by governors was minimal. The governors left it very much to the head to 'flag up' concerns, and regarded themselves as a sounding board at best.

This is still the case in many instances and schools survive quite happily. However, though this sort of minimal input leaves some heads to get on with running the school without undue meddling, which may seem highly desirable, the fact of governors taking too much of a back seat leaves the school without desirable energy and perspective. For example, though one head was pleased to have virtually totally delegated powers over staffing, the involvement of governors in appointments – shortlisting for some posts and interviewing – does bring them into contact with values and policies as they are happening on the ground. It puts flesh on the skeleton. All Impington governors will at some point be involved with staff appointments and though they never wish to usurp professional judgement they do contribute a great deal, enjoy the process and gain insights which would be impossible to convey any other way. Sharing tasks allows an ongoing conversation and relationship. It allows, too, an opportunity to get applied philosophy across.

Where the head is clear about his or her aims and values, s/he can influence appointments professionally, enjoying the added perspective of interested governors. In 12 years of headship I can recall only once when a governor reminded me rather emphatically that, 'It is the governors who decide.' He then decided after a raised eyebrow, however, that he wanted me to have ultimate say!

Stressed heads and anxious governors

However, the fear of, or the fact of, interference does stress some heads and there has been in some situations understandable avoidance of engaging governors too fully in issues; and governors, too, while pleased to be governors, and perhaps in some instances while enjoying the status of the position, have not wanted to be too overloaded by the complexities of the system. There is also a sense of inadequacy about understanding all the ins and outs of an ever-changing school system: the professional language is off-putting and mystifying when sometimes the actual issues are not. Indeed, many governors were most modest and fearful of their ignorance as more than one interviewee highlighted. One chairperson asked me to temper my questions accordingly:

> If you could target your questions so that you lead me into what you want me to say. I always make the point whenever I am talking to someone that basically speaking I am a businessman; I know very little about education. I know which way I like to see the school going, but I cannot give you a technical answer, I can only give you a 'feeling' answer. Although I hope I do the job fairly well I am not convinced that I am the best man for the job. I am not a professional.

Yet, on asking him what he enjoyed about the job he answered:

> I must be honest – it is selfishness really. It is something totally different to what I do in my normal day. It is like a form of relaxation in a way. That is why I say it is selfish. And obviously I have become very fond of the school ... because I know the majority of the staff personally, and we all get on well. It is a happy school, and it is something nice to be involved with.

The problem today is that more than this diffident and well-meaning stance may be required and many parents and community members are giving up, fearing the workload and feeling inadequate to the task.

If governors of quality and goodwill are to be encouraged to stay on and to assume the greater responsibilities which independence will thrust upon them, then it is essential that heads in particular think out the sort of working mode which is most appropriate to that new independence. It is a mode which must retain some sense of fun. If all governors' concerns relate to woe rather than weal then they, too, are likely to exit.

Defensive heads may wish to blind governors with science and create a dependency culture; others may genuinely be overzealous in the information they supply. Deciding on the right amount and pitch of information is an important task for the head, for the quality of policy which follows will be in direct proportion to the quality of guidance.

The management skills of chairs of governors

It is important that the whole governing body is well informed. Within the survey there was considerable evidence of chairs of governors in particular bearing the brunt of much of the strategic thinking involved, and supporting the head often in the role of a close friend rather than simply a colleague. This assumption of responsibility can cause a dependency culture in other governors and even if the chair's stance results from existing apathy, this will not be improved if other governors are allowed to drift. One chair described her exasperation with the passenger governors who had not woken up, as she seemed to have done, to the extent of their responsibilities. I asked her whether the other governors could do more to help her:

> There are about four who will do that. The rest ... You have a parish priest here who is a very nice man but he has only been here just over a year. We have a Labour councillor who will spend half the meeting telling you how the unions would have done it. As far as I am concerned, I don't want politics in a governors' meeting ... We are all, hopefully, intelligent people. [I might say:] 'I want a reaction to this.' [The reply might be:] 'Write a letter. We'll leave it to you – you're the chair.' They will sit there and spout forth for two or three hours, but at the end of the day, I feel that they have no sense at all.

The same point was made by another chair who was enthusiastically involved in her school, while some governors were more what she termed 'professional committee people'. She recognized at the same time, however, that the role is voluntary and increasingly demanding, therefore parents or people with some sort of real interest in education were more likely, she felt, to be more active and truly sympathetic:

> We tried to co-opt a bank manager, an architect – people that had knowledge that we needed but did not have. I think people tend to forget that a governing body is a voluntary position. It is very demanding now, and I don't think you can possibly have a commitment unless you are really interested in education or you are a parent, who cares not just about your children's education, but about everybody's.

In this school the head and chair worked closely together to move information between committees so that all governors were *au fait* with discussions and recommended decisions before the main business meetings.

Governor as expert

Expertise is, of course, important and useful but if governors feel they cannot see the wood for the trees then they will soon feel impotent and resign. This fact was clearly recognized by one chair:

> CHAIR: One of the main problems when you start as a new governor is that you think you have to become an expert in education. But that is a big mistake. What is needed is good management, obtaining an overview ... what do they actually bring into the school as an individual? Do they come as empty vessels to be filled? What they do have is a belief in their own expertise, and this is channelled into sub-committees, so that they feel they have a purpose: property and finance, personnel, curriculum. So they feel that they have some expertise which is relevant.
>
> SW: ... harnessing people for their strengths, and to some extent, making sure that they are not overwhelmed by the dross/paperwork so they don't become disenchanted with being a governor.
>
> CHAIR: When I first came here there was a new emphasis on 'getting the governors trained' and bringing them up with all the new legislation. Many of the governors I chatted to were drowning in paper. Every time we went to our postboxes there was another wad of paper from the LEA. We can't read it all. But when we got down

to the nitty-gritty of what we needed and wanted to know, essentially there was very little. We have ... professional advisers ... What we can bring to the school are lateral thinking, clear management minds, who haven't over the years been weighed down with all the bureaucracy.

Building the team

Beyond the matter of managing the 'how' of informing the governors there is also the management of the governing body as a team. It may, of course, suit a chair who enjoys considerable scope not to encourage too much involvement, in the same way as it was suggested it might suit a head. The legal requirements of school governance do discourage an abuse of a chair's discretion, for except in cases of urgency or emergency the main body does have to approve most decisions. Nevertheless, in practice a powerful or active chair can hold considerable sway, encouraging, perhaps unconsciously, apathy or disempowerment of more diffident colleagues. If chairs allow themselves to become the mainstay, making decisions and partnering the head through thick and thin, this may be a comfortable and pleasant position for both parties, but it is not an educative position. In some cases chairs explained that they supported the head against governors who doubted the head's philosophy – but often the conflict was not brought out into the open, but absorbed or deflected.

If the chair is managing the governing body then s/he should try to face conflict, aided by the head. Evasion or tacit riding of division undermines what should be the main support of the school: the governing body as watchdog and advocate. To get the most out of any governing body it is essential that the head and the chair build a team. One chair realized this very clearly and described how he had set about achieving this objective. There had been some difference of viewpoint in this body, in fact, which had not come fully into the open; the underlying tension had affected the relationships within the governing body and there were undeclared views on how the school should best be run:

The problem we have is that as a governing body we meet irregularly, you are a collection of strangers, you rarely know anybody, you are a jumble of people from all sorts of backgrounds

... but no team. The most important thing about a governing body is that at least it should be a team. Because of the politics that is not always totally possible. Three of us went to a team-building exercise ... We recognize that if you do not get the team right you will never win anything. Identify the problem, get to know each other and dispel the unwritten, hidden agenda.

The initial training day for three developed into a bigger session for the other governors apart from three problematic members. The chair explained:

We all got there. No trouble apart from three, who were the main problematic governors. But it was better to have 15 working together rather than none working together ... what I think we are coming round to now much more is that we have got to deal with each other's values, and the managing of those values. In your governing body as regards the conflict what you have got is different values which are either not at the moment being declared, or they don't 'sit'. We need to tackle that rather than ignore it. So part of the management challenge is actually to find a way to make people face up to the issues of values.

In nine or ten months' time we will be faced with the challenge of 50 or 60 per cent of the existing governors going ... I said to [the head] that in my view it is vital that during the first meeting of the new governing body, that they agree what they actually want to achieve. What do they want as a school?

Of course, the management of teams requires skill, insight and time which this chair, a parent governor, clearly was prepared to put in. However, not all chairs would have such skills and there was evidence of chairs preferring to work with some of the governing body and/or the head alone. It was clear that there was often an intended paternalism on the part of the chair, compounded by a lack of challenge from other members. One county councillor and chair of long-standing gave something of the flavour of this:

I find most governors these days don't want to get too much involved in the actual day-to-day running of the school. They are supportive if it is said to them, 'Look, we are in difficulty financially,' and they would say then, 'How do you suggest we handle it? What support do you need? Do we need to make representations?' I always try to lead the governing body to be a supportive element, to be there when needed when the battle is on or anything. Supportive if things are going wrong, or if there is an incident, or anything like that. But not to manage. Because I think we appoint and pay professionals to do that job.

Sometimes chairs who had been quite autocratic were remembered with mixed feelings, for although they had reigned with a strong hand, they had at least fought for the school, as one interviewee nostalgically recalled:

X was the chair who retired before the beginning of this four-year session, and I actually joined when he was chair. He was famous, if not notorious, for running a tight ship and having the absolute classic conventional governors' meeting that was a rubber stamp for everything. He relied on the school staff to do everything, and if they didn't he would jump. He was there every day, he was monitoring what was happening, and he would tell us, 'That's okay, you can get that through,' and I used to think it will be good to move into a situation where we have much more time to get to know what is happening and to really be a part of it. We looked forward to that.

In today's climate not only is there a need for a collaborative ethic within governing bodies but, as I will emphasize in the next chapter, between governing bodies. Inevitably in a real world much of the facilitating of this team-building effort will fall on heads who see it as important. It points, too, to the need for some head and governor training to be be done together, but heads and chairs would perhaps be best advised not to rely too heavily on outside courses. In addressing their particular and local needs it may well be better to manage as much group training for all governors in-house, involving a professional input as appropriate. What is important in such training is that governors consider procedures and codes of working together and that unidentified value-differences which may otherwise fester are brought out into the light of day. This requires a bold style of head and chair, but in the long run must lead to a more cohesive and honest team, which, if nothing else, has been bonded by voice.

A use of time

Certainly such thinking and strategy were evident in some schools in the survey. One had, with some facilitation from the local authority, set up a team-building day to look at values. It was relatively successful but, having agreed to give up a Sunday, there was annoyance on the part of some governors that the course overran and a suggestion was made that they should reconvene for an evening, as my interviewee explained:

> GOVERNOR: What we did last year was to have an entire day [a Sunday] when we all got together and the idea was that we would get to know each other better and talk about just these issues ... [these had to do with the values and realization of the values of the college].
>
> SW: Was that just governors ...?
>
> GOVERNOR: Governors plus the executive members of staff. We had a facilitator from County Hall, and away we went. We met, and we had some ideas, identified aims and objectives and all the rest of it. In fact, we were rather disappointed that having had a professional facilitator she didn't really force us into having to come to either conclusions or an agenda by 4 o'clock. (We had all agreed we would stay until 4 o'clock.) She actually made a terrible error, because she said in this kindly, neutral, open way, 'Perhaps we could stay for another half-hour in order to sort out these last things.' I was really astonished; people were really cross. They said, 'No, we had agreed to come until 4 o'clock and this is the time we were given, and that is that, we will now break up, because some people have other commitments.'

The day was, of course, a very good idea, but what is interesting is the governors' reaction to extra time, for it highlights the way any volunteer, unless he or she is extremely motivated, is likely to react. The governors felt quite noble in having given up a Sunday but they have other lives. This is why inevitably the head, and perhaps an enthusiastic chair, have to choreograph and manage the rest of the body as they would any team. Time management has to be a consideration, not least in the interest of the staff, too, for it is in nobody's interest to become jaded and worn out. The management of information, team and time, therefore, figures very highly, as it should do in all management. It figures more when dealing with volunteers.

Governors are also more likely to go on courses in their own time when the invitation is a personal rather than blanket one and where the costs incurred are met from the school budget. Attending conferences with members of staff also reassures and allows dialogue and creative thinking to start in partnership. Sharing INSET days also builds relationships and this again adds to a sense of team.

Letting the children motivate the volunteer

The chair who set up a team-building exercise recognized how his head actually tapped the strengths of the team, getting them to participate in areas where they could feel confident. There is also a need to bring them closer to the actual working of the school – through a school visit, for example. This is when they are more inclined to forget time. My own governors enjoy the visits immensely and even find school lunch tolerable, which no doubt some students would maintain says a great deal for their fortitude or their usual fare. Impington governors come in as a group on visiting days and are linked up with a student or take part in the student council. A discussion this year between governors and students about whether boys needed to wear ties was sufficiently decisive for the council to put their thrust into other modifications to the uniform. The perceived conservatism of staff was qualified by the evident equal conservatism of adults 'from beyond' whose views as members of the 'real' world are always more credible. The governors supported ties which staff found helpful. Of course, the absolute rights and wrongs of the school insisting on this aspect of uniform are another matter and no doubt the question will arise again next year. One cannot help but reflect that it would be useful to time the governors' visit with next year's uniform review again!

Bringing youngsters into meetings also brings home the feel of the school, as do taking part in interviews or counselling of students. If governors are to be encouraged to stand up for their school they must have some sense of pride, usefulness and ownership. The more smitten they become with the excitement, fun and tears of the place the more readily they will turn out to attend meetings and to think carefully how they might help. Children talking to governors are refreshing and a great motivator.

A personalized view

The importance of this closeness to the school's concrete processes rather than having a sole focus on the abstraction of school information was endorsed by both heads and chairs. Parent governors or former parent governors, contrary to the often common fear that parents tend to be too self-interested, were seen to have the compensatory aspect of really knowing the school and having some concern for it, which brings one back to the theme of personal response and particularity. In the same way that parents and students need to be seen and treated as individuals and to be enabled to develop the most personal connection possible with a school, governors need a similar opportunity.

Obviously, the existence of current and former parents on governing bodies may well be an enriching factor rather than a hindrance but the fact remains that this may not always fit with reality or the school's needs. Ways must be found, therefore, to draw in the 'passengers' and professional committee people in such a way that they can really contribute. A governing body requires as much people management as any other team connected with the school. The pivot in managing all the various teams of a school is often the head, who in the new climate may have to relinquish the more reassuring areas where s/he feels comfortable and potent, such as teaching on a regular basis, to concentrate on these important constituents in the new educational world.

In other words, the governing bodies must be managed as every other aspect of the school is managed but they must be managed with a view to empowerment not control. The real control lies in the steering of the teams and the development of the people, and possibly on occasion the confronting of people whose personal and political agendas are getting in the way. This is easier to do where those issues are on the open agenda rather than hidden in the woodwork. Governing bodies must therefore get their houses more in order if autonomous schools are to be well supported. They must, too, learn to manage values in their policy making, encouraging value-differences to come into the open so that they can be better explored. The head must enable governors to see those values both in the context of the real life of the school and the political decisions affecting that life.

It is, in fact, in this latter realm that the vast majority of governors can feel that they are in uncharted waters. However, despite the assertions of politicians like John Butcher that schools should be freed from the political background, the governance of education cannot be divorced from politics, though it does not need to become riven by party political feuding. In the new circumstances of schools, governors are inevitably caught up in the decisions made by politicians, and all schools will in future need to shift for themselves in the area of school advocacy. The awakening and anxiety surrounding this area came through clearly in the survey and will be addressed in the next chapter.

Chapter 7

The Politicization of Governing Bodies

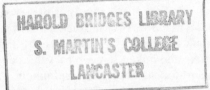
Politics fill vacuum

The *Times Educational Supplement* (1 May 1992) shouted the headline: 'Politics Poised To Fill Vacuum', and reporters went on to say:

> Governors' meetings are set to become a battleground this autumn as new members force through job cuts and steer schools towards opting out. There are fears that reluctance among ordinary parents to take up their fair share of governor vacancies will leave the way clear for the political parties to pack bodies with their own activists.

There has been considerable speculation in recent times as to whether schools would have sufficient people coming forward as governors, given the greater responsibilities which so much change has placed on the shoulders of these volunteers. The prospect of an exodus of ordinary members of the public could pave the way, it has been felt, for political activists to dominate new bodies as they reconstitute, or failing that, that schools could find governing bodies dominated by the retired and semi-retired.

Of course, schools have good retired people and are glad of the time they give, but it is not healthy for an institution serving the needs of the young to have only such volunteers. Political activism, similarly, is not necessarily a bad thing but no head would relish more than his or her fair share. The governing body needs a mix of people of all ages and active walks of life if it is to reflect the profile of communities.

A politicized role

Though political activism may develop in some parts of the country it is perhaps more the case that governors themselves are having to become more politically aware, because the *role* is being more *politicized*. The effect of Government reforms has been to put education higher on the public agenda than ever before. Governors and parents have been gradually waking up to quite radical changes for which they are not wholly prepared. The same mix of views obtains over changes to local schools as it does over the fact of hospitals operating as businesses and running their own affairs. Both health and education are very personal matters and linked to people's values and ideals and thus changes of this sort touch people very profoundly. As the public wakes up to the implications of the reforms, a variety of emotions and reactions inevitably focus on governing bodies: will GM schools gain resources at the expense of other schools and will GM or the introduction of Magnet Schools (these specialize in a particular subject area such as Music, Science, Technology) alter admissions in an area in such a way as to deny children access to their traditionally local school?

Governors as much as parents have often been puzzled or dismayed at the suggestion of dismantling a democratic local system administered by locally elected members. Debates have in some areas been bitter, in others apathetic, depending on the local circumstances and tradition. Governors are inevitably at the heart of this debate as heads have attempted to remain professionally neutral. Beyond the questions about Grant-Maintained Status which are more recent and current, governors have to face the fact that educational reforms and changes do give rise to political or community concerns, be they minor or major. Education continues to be high on the national agenda and this state of affairs is not likely to go away. The move towards autonomous schools puts governors firmly in the hot seat which can be both exhilarating and exceptionally controversial. Non-activists are suddenly having to be activated and are in the public eye. Newspaper reporters will want to know the views of governing bodies on any political decision and, indeed, already seek press statements if they know that public interest items are on the governors' agenda, such as discussions of GMS or funding cuts, to name but two.

When governors were interviewed on this issue, which clearly links with the management of values (ie the value context as it impacts upon the school), different states of readiness and awareness were apparent. A growing political awareness was evident in the reflections of governors grappling with so much in transition. It was evident that governors were being woken from a nominal responsibility to a real one, as schools become increasingly independent of local planning and control. The change of expectations, and the problems some governors are having in adapting to that change, were given very clear expression by a saddened chair of governors; she could see the size of the task and had become a governor because as a parent she had found her school body faceless and ineffective. However, despite even the shake-ups of the reforms, she still had not been able to galvanize them to any great extent, which meant a great deal fell to her and the head:

I have been a governor for fifteen years – I am like one of the antiques! It came about really through me being, I suppose, if you like, impetuous. It was at a PTA meeting when my own children were here. Very little got done. Governors were faceless people, you never got to meet them in those days. You never knew what was going on ... But they had been governors for years, a lot of them professional people ... there was never any policy for the school ... We were reading through some of the old minutes recently, and it seemed to me a glorified tea-party. You came in, and it was like putting on your mantle for an hour and a half. You never saw anybody again for six months. Nobody ever contacted you. You came perhaps to the governors' prize-giving. Apart from that nothing. Then of course ... we started the weekly newsletter, so at least you got to know what was going on. But even now there is still some apathy.

This apathy, which a relatively new head had been seeking to remedy, highlights the starkness of the change required in attitudes and commitment of some governors. If one adds on to such inertia the political whirlwind of change today it does not suggest a readiness and preparedness in all governing bodies to meet the political implications of their role.

Continuity and change

Despite areas of weakness, there are many governors who are coping well with the challenges and the good thing in all the changes taking place is that it is proving to be a catalyst for bodies pulling together and thinking about educational values and political issues constructively. This may have its stressful side but it is also healthy. Though many governors have no experience of public life or the skills needed to negotiate in the public arena, they are learning them fast and are more truly engaged *precisely because* they are needed. Several of my own governors, for example, have decided to stay on for a further term of office to see the school through the changes of the 1990s. They want to help the school and know that a period of continuity is needed, particularly if the school goes grant-maintained. Values need to be carried forward and safeguarded through possible turbulence. The present governors are responsible for choosing the first governors if we become a GMS school, and they would want to have a part in determining the sorts of people who might be established or co-opted for the next five or seven years to pass on a legacy of cherished values: it is a question of linking the best of the past to the best of a future.

Political awakening

Schools in the past have seemed stable and conservative institutions, changing gradually within local collective values which have been built on an assumption of political continuity and stability in our culture, which many people have seen as immutable. The fact of political/value controversy popping up in established and steady institutions like schools and hospitals has proved a great surprise for many governors and parents, and they have reacted initially rather sluggishly. One chair of governors gave an instance of this when he described the efforts of a local feeder school to go grant-maintained. This was before the General Election of 1992. The parents reacted slowly and then debate gathered incredible momentum as parents fought the move, leaving the governors, who were pushing for the change, with a very emphatic 'no' vote.

British culture is attuned to gentle, not dramatic, change in our institutions and thus the public tends to be slow to react to the sort of shake-up which some aspects of the reforms are presenting. There is often an inertia in our institutions which needs 'friendly bombs', rather like those proposed by Sir John Betjeman to fall on Slough. However, the effect of the reforms has been to blow up structures to such an extent that it is worrying to contemplate where the fragments will fall and in what constellation.

Slow reactions also relate to the fact that in British culture there is a particular aversion to the word 'political' which one does not find in countries such as France or Germany. In the British culture it tends to be a term which needs some explanation before it is sufficiently sanitized. However, to be politically aware or active is not necessarily to be politically subversive or fanatical, but rather to take appropriate action or decisions in the light of political issues which affect everyday life. As the main determinants now of schools' policies, governing bodies are inevitably politicized by the fact that they are having to respond to political decisions and are now making decisions which affect whole communities.

It is, however, politicization as a general term; it is politics with, as the British often preface the word to avoid offence, a small 'p': that is to say that if politics as a concept is defined as the moral and economic basis of social decisions, then schools are inevitably caught up in this, and governors as policy-makers with the head, who is often also a governor, are the guardians of the institution's good and its integrity. At all events, the reforms do constitute political direction of education, with which the public is inevitably engaged, for all children are in some way affected by the changes. The reforms constitute not the end of a process but the beginning of one. The Government's agenda is provoking discussion and a slow awakening of political response in all concerned in the issues. The process of shaking inertia and traditionally conservative institutions asunder may well be providing the agenda for a reconstruction of the service, as values and energies which have lain dormant are forced to the fore. Educational questions are today's 'high agenda' media fodder and, though reporting is variable, the focus at least is healthy.

Governors as watchdogs and advocates

The active involvement of governors is not likely to go away, for all schools are now much more directly accountable to their communities for the decisions they take. Opted-out schools in particular will not have the intermediary of local government, and governors and parents will need to influence central government if they have concerns over budgets or local planning. Governors will need to court parent support and know how to put pressure on politicians effectively in working actively for their school. One governor described how her waking up to this point had initially raised laughter from other governor colleagues at the end of governor training day:

> At the end of our day ... I actually said to somebody who made a point about how do we all know that we share these views, that I didn't think that mattered. But what I thought was absolutely key for any governor was to be able to know the enemy. They all burst out laughing, and could not understand what I was talking about. I felt the executive understood what I meant. I said, 'Well, the local authority might be the enemy. It looks to me as though that is what we need to know about, that they are going to be constantly pressing us to economize and we are going to be constantly pressing to expand.' They couldn't see this, but it seems to me that if you don't understand that, then I think it is a barrier to generating the kind of values [we think are important]. For if you are not willing to say that the quality of the learning experience we are offering to these children is such a priority that we are going to resist any attempt from anywhere else to constrain the quality, then unless you know how to fight, unless you know how to hold your corner in personnel or curriculum or whatever ... Now, some do understand that; I have a feeling when I said it at that moment they thought I was being ridiculously dramatic.

Such language is, of course, combative, as one might expect of governors feeling possibly concerned that they may be facing the strength of a political process with which they are not familiar, but whether such feeling will mellow into more confident and sophisticated response only time and experience will tell. The significant factor in her point and the way that it was made, is that the political context is something which more governors and parents are recognizing and engaging with.

Surviving in a tough climate

A similarly dawning awareness of the political questions emerging with the new and apparently unencumbered freedoms of the White Paper's 'choice and diversity', was expressed by the chair of another governing body, who could see in the school's own internal harmony a lack of sufficient abrasion to put governors and staff on their mettle where some issues were concerned. In other words, this school was more intent on friendship than on dealing with anything inimical to its survival. He had enjoyed, and still did enjoy, supporting the school, though he admitted that the changes had made it less fun. He felt the reforms expected too much of volunteers like himself who had a full-time job besides. He had wanted to be a generally supportive and encouraging associate rather than a professional governor, as it were. The job, he recognized now, needed to develop a greater sharpness and grit in its oyster, in its view of itself and the issues affecting it from outside, if it was to prosper in the new competitive world of the reforms.

He had been chair for many years and had enormous pleasure and pride in the school. Well supported by the LEA in the past, the school had had little contact with anything or anyone adverse. It was a school used to working in harmony with itself and the local authority. Now its 'ecology' had been severely upset by changes such as open enrolment and formula budgeting and suddenly the internal congruence found less sympathetic relationship with the world outside. Parents seemed to be turning to more traditional schools, despite the happy and harmonious atmosphere of the school which did its very best for the pupils it served.

The chair, then, was recognizing that the harmony and niceness of the school could be a weakness as well as a strength, for there was not the habit, perhaps, of dealing with political questions and problems which were increasingly affecting the school. The school's culture and that of the political climate did not sit easily together, and part of him wanted to protest against what was happening to education for, in his view, it was adversely affecting the school. He found himself, however, unable to raise issues effectively within the governing body: the reaction of other governors and the head was that he was being too political.

The embarrassment about political discussion was dominant even though certain subjects needed an airing to decide how the conflicting cultures were to be managed. The situation frustrated the chair considerably for he felt some reaction should come from the governors on behalf of the school. The same aversion to political discussion affected other subjects which needed facing up to. The internal harmony eschewed tension. We drew out his thoughts further:

sw: [The harmony] is certainly impressive. I think the degree of unity which comes over in terms of what the governors want and what the staff want is very impressive. Listening today, and you have already expressed it ... the greatest danger is ... that you don't have tension. It is good for you to have a countering point somewhere down the line, because when people are so unified they can actually become, not complacent, but perhaps unaware of the dangers or not abreast of what is happening.

GOVERNOR: I think that is very true, and I think the great danger is the fact that you tend to believe everything you are told. I don't distrust the staff, but they are bound to have their biases, and so we have got to be able to see beyond that. You need to have somebody who can see beyond what is being said, in other words reading between the lines ... I personally think we ought to be doing a lot more than we are. But every time I say so people are wary – it's too political. There are a number of times when I could have screamed. I'm talking about us personally, not nationally ... [The head] is very frightened of upsetting the apple-cart of our situation in the area.

Harmony: a lotus flower

The harmony, therefore, tended to blind governors and staff to possible flaws in their own midst and excluded also the mention of politics, for this again was an area of potential dissonance. Indeed, schools which concentrate on value-congruence to too great a degree are in danger of lotus eating. In a competitive and distrustful climate it is not for school management to breed cynicism and hard-nosed tactics, but it behoves any school to be alert to its weaknesses and any 'enemy', as the governor earlier put it, if it is to survive. The chair was glad in fact that they now had on the governing body one governor who made them think, though he had to admit to twitching a bit in his seat when this man spoke. Nevertheless, he recognized that he was asking incisive questions that the school needed to ask itself and thus he recognized the need for this tension for the health of the school's psyche and well-being.

However, in both incisive questioning and political response, the school needed to work out its position. The head's resistance to political responses, which one chair mentioned, no doubt had to do not with a wish to suppress political discussion but with a fear that any discussion would lead to an inept reaction. Professionals can experience a sense of unease at community members dabbling in politics, for this can rebound on establishments, particularly in a culture like ours, where politics is often a pejorative term and people generally are wary of such talk and action.

Thus, professionals and governors need to iron out what might be the appropriate responses to the chair's wish for action, or the previous governor's exhortation to 'know the enemy'. Political skills, how to employ and acquire them, rather than feelings about them, need to be on the governing body's agenda. Letting feeling as an expression of values emerge, however, need not embarrass us as much as it does, provided some ground rules of discussion have been set. Political values are part of the *value narrative* of our lives and school leadership has to facilitate that narrative rather than suppress it. If the school starts with its values then any political decision can be viewed not as party political but as adding or taking away from the school's own plan. Within this area some resolution or compromise has to be found.

People, not systems, are responsible

In the market culture governors' policies become much more politically loaded because they are not working within any agreed moral framework but are balancing the various values of a web of social and political relationships and emphases. Where there is a common framework for social affairs, where justice and quality of life are more constitutionally determined, then the populace at large have fewer moral dilemmas to face in the public realm. Where, however, moral decisions are devolved more directly to individuals through a system of market forces, then people either have to think, negotiate and act more deeply in ethical and political ways, or, in submitting to the logic of the system as a determinant of value, refuse to think rigorously of its demands at all. However, as Greenfield (1986, p 71) writes, 'it is people who are responsible for organizations' (and systems) 'and people who change them. Organizations have reality only through human action, and it is that action (and the human will driving it) that we must come to understand.'

The complexity of values and competition in a market does not alter that fact, it simply makes the consensus more difficult, because competition either causes polarity or forces compromise rather than integrity. Thus, in a society which politically legitimates competition, governors who have responsibility for school decisions are bound to meet some controversy. Governors may want to blame the system, but they will be held responsible as agents of choice if little or no thought is apparent and little or no action is negotiated.

So, rather than escaping the political background, governors and heads are more directly caught up in politics. Local government is less the focus of decisions affecting schools: it is governors who are now the arbitrators of value and policy within a market culture legitimated by Government policies. Accountable to parents and, as a GMS school, more directly to the Secretary of State for Education, governors' understanding of political process and points of influence becomes a major competence. If schools are inadequately funded, teachers and parents will look to governors to remedy the situation. Governors will have to discover new powers of pressure and influence.

A political voice

Schools have traditionally been pleased to have local councillors on the governing body because it has often been a way to gain insight into how planning and resourcing of the service are going and a channel for influencing that process. Clearly if the powers of local government in education are to diminish, and they are diminishing already to a considerable extent, local political contact, though still helpful, is less important than access to national policy-makers and purse-holders. Governors need to have influence on national plans for education and its resourcing, for, unlike the private sector of schooling where governors determine fees and building programmes, state school governors manage an *allocation* of resources which is determined by governmental political process, not generated by fees or other income. Thus, access to political representatives and pressure on those representatives has to be an effective part of governor strategy.

Parent power

The Secretary of State for Education has seen in the turnout of parents for GMS ballots a greater commitment to schools than local elections demonstrate, suggesting that parental interest in self-managing schools is a substitute for local government. He sees parents impacting much more on local schools through GMS than they did through the LEAs: he sees parents making schools stronger and fitter in every way.

Inevitably, this must involve strength, too, in acquiring resources and building programmes as appropriate. Therefore, it is increasingly to parents that governors are turning and will turn for help in lobbying Members of Parliament and key politicians. Parent power has already been mobilized in many areas in a collective way and campaigns, while not always effective, have provided a strong voice to Government on school needs.

Governors will need not only to engage more closely with the school's own constituency but networks of governor and parent pressure groups are already emerging in many areas and are likely to continue to do so if all schools, whatever their type and character, find themselves underfunded. More political negotiation will have to be dealt with by the school's own community and where schools have causes in common, such as budgetary and, possibly in the future, curriculum issues, then collective voice is likely to be needed and sought. Of course, this is another time-consuming role for governors to take on – hence the concern or assumption by many that ordinary and well-meaning governors might be replaced by political activists.

New impetus for governors and communities

However, another more optimistic view is that the greater engagement needed in education will be an impetus for many 'ordinary' governors – whatever ordinary might mean – to do something for their school and children. The greater reliance which schools are likely to have on the active involvement of their stakeholders could lead to a sense of common purpose in governors and parents alike. Despite the greater political control of education, educational values will have to be worked through at the local level. Indeed, such local purpose might find something of a safeguard in GMS against *political activism* as opposed to *activated political values*: schools with a strong identity and prized values may be more likely to hold on to those values under GMS, for governors themselves appoint the first or foundation governors who serve for five or seven years.

Of course, local commitment and enthusiasm may still not produce 'good' or 'enlightened' values in schools, for any judgement as to the worthwhileness of values is relative. In a market culture and pluralist society, however, nothing can be guaranteed where values are concerned. Until we are able as a country to establish a common

constitutional value-framework for education, good values and practice rely on management which has a healthy openness to modification
and public discernment. It is these which require public attention and
improvement.

In the short and medium term, good practice and example have to be
fostered by the cumulative process of the collective 'professional
college' mentioned in Chapter 3. This has always been the case in
education and until we achieve, as I have said, a constitutionally
agreed framework for state education, it will always be so. Indeed,
many would justifiably argue that local frameworks are safer and more
manageable than central ones: I have indicated already the anxiety
over value monopoly. If local frameworks are to work, however, there
does need to be some form of federalism to avoid parochialism. Heads
and governors need to encourage such links in their more isolated
positions.

An examination of values

No school is safe either from political activists or from values which are
too particular to local or historical conditions. The best safeguard for
any latent consensus on values and practice has to be the examination
of values as a dynamic and ongoing process in our educational
establishments. Governors need to recognize that they are caught up
in the nexus of social and political relationships and consider what their
values and strategies are to be in terms of that position. Giving in to
inept silence or placing heads in sand will not move schools on very far.

In terms of their political and social remit, governors too need to
consider what influence and power networks can be of use and help to
the school. Governors' own contacts and expertise can be tapped and,
through the wider contact with parents, similar support built up.
Governors' local forums and Parent Association Federations have
formed themselves in the past and are likely to bring excellent
collective voice and expertise. The Secretary of State for Education is
right to see in local involvement of parents in schools a livelier prospect
for schools to become stronger. All school stakeholders have,
however, to be willing to be involved with each other and the business
of education for this to prove a viable alternative to local government
voice.

The de-anonymizing of politics

The willingness to become involved will not stem from abstract rhetoric or exhortation. The real instigators and motivators of will and action in adults are likely to be the children, if their voice is heard. Often the silent partners in all this talk of politics and budgets, the children are the reason for the efforts of all other participants in education. They are the real spokespersons for schools and their spokesmanship resides not in any conscious part they should be made to play but in heads and teachers simply helping the public at large to hear their natural voice in work and play.

Children as persons merit more of our attention. In the selling, promoting and buying of the market place, and in political change, children are, despite the rhetoric, anonymized and schematized; they disappear from view as persons and become pawns in a game. Under increasing pressure to perform in tests and examinations, students can be ignored as interesting, thoughtful and needy persons in their own right. Budgets, parental ballots, curriculum assessment and organizational change can easily screen the children from us. Schools are about the actual experience of children caught up as much as anyone, not only in recent education changes, but in life in general, with their share of problems and dilemmas to bear. Adults, and this includes *us* the professionals, who allow themselves the opportunity to listen to young people, see the rhetoric of change in a different light.

Focusing on children and values which promote their general good is likely to draw particular support not only for any individual school from its community, but also for the universal values of education, through their being given human and personal shape in the children. This closer focus on persons, not cyphers, must influence political decisions to a greater extent. There has been in the history of all nations, including our own, too much emphasis on fitting people to systems and ideologies. Schools must help to combat these anonymizing tendencies. Governors and parents need to understand education in a personal way if they are to marshal their will and commitment to political skills in making children's real needs the basis of decisions. The next chapter looks at ways in which schools can help to make young people's voices heard.

Chapter 8

The 'X' Factor – Schools Fit For Children

A more personal response

Since the 1944 Act, politicians and educationalists have pointed to various sorts of school organization which are purportedly in the interest of each child. In reality no system has proved completely ideal but rather better or worse than others. Though there are grave reservations about the fairness and effectiveness of the Government's reforms, particularly among professionals, they have struck a significant chord with parts of the public who want to see a shift away from general to particular responses to their children: the more exigent section of the parent population want to have the personally tailored response to their children which it is believed fee-paying schools will provide.

Indeed, ostensibly in response to this growing expectation for state education, the Government wants to model state education on the customer ethic of the private system which it sees as more attentive to parents' wishes; the fact of self-governing schools also obviates the costs of further bureaucracy such as local authorities. It is a system which moves away from state paternalism to one designed to satisfy those who can exercise their rights. Support for those parents who are unable or unwilling to do so is passed over in any literature, as is an emphasis on parental responsibility. It is schools which are seen to be accountable for attendance rates and, generally, pupil behaviour.

What is the 'X' factor?

It is therefore naturally of interest to all schools to know if there are particular ingredients which concerned parents are looking for in a school. If these could be defined, then school leaders would at least be able to take considered account of such views in their planning and attention to quality. They could also respond to such expectations with a professional voice, seeking to refine and modify them in the interests of the children where they consider it appropriate. The head of an independent school attempted to define what it is that parents want from a school in his explanation of why, as he put it, even 'card carrying members of the Labour Party' will tell him the torture they suffer to their principles in choosing private education because of something he termed the 'X' factor:

> HEAD: What I have picked up, and what I think has been confirmed by one or two independent surveys, is that yes, parents want a high academic standard, but actually they want an 'X' factor which is terribly hard to put one's finger on. It's an amalgam: they want their child loved, they actually want to feel that somebody cares about the child; it doesn't matter whether he is a genius or at the bottom. They want him structured. They actually want him to know what he is expected to do ... it also has to be said that quite a lot of parents are looking for the grammar school they went to, but can't find ... within the state sector.
>
> SW: So there is a sort of security they are looking for, that gives off the signals that they had.
>
> HEAD: They may well be looking for the security that they had. They would justify it by saying, 'I went to this school – loved it – I am grateful to it – and I want my child to have the same experience.'

The drive for such security which may indeed emanate from their own schooling, or from the schooling they did not have but would have liked to have had, leads many parents to overcome their scruples about paying for education. Fears that their child might not be stretched and nostalgia overcome their wishes to wear the social 'white hat', as the independent head revealed:

> About 60 per cent of our 11-year-old entry are dragged into [private] education; they would rather not come, including the parent who said, 'I will give three cheers when my son leaves [your school] after

seven years because what I have done by signing on with you is to condemn myself to seven years of not owning up as to where my son is being educated at any supper or drinks party which I am liable to attend.

Reflecting upon this 'X' factor it is not difficult to recognize that what is being described is common also to the expectation of parents of state schools. In choosing a school parents do want good academic standards but, equally, they want a high level of interest in the child as an individual: a concern for his or her personal academic and moral growth and potential. They want, too, the child to be happy and this they see in the structure and care being exerted and expressed in the relationships between child and staff, and staff and parents. In the state sector many parents still worry about making a fuss, but all parents tend to be roused if any injustice or neglect affects *their* child. Any discipline which evidently does not 'see' the child as a person is quickly and rightly criticized. In other words, teachers cannot apply the sort of rough justice that often obtained in schools in the past.

Parenting

At the same time, there is often a guilt in parents that they are not spending enough time with, and giving sufficient love to, the child, and in their busy lives they expect the school to compensate. When things go wrong that guilt may turn not on the child or back on the family but on the school for having in some way failed the child. This tendency is certainly given encouragement in the White Paper: it is schools which must not fail pupils and it is schools which must ensure all manner of parental responsibilities which could be considered a normal expectation of parenting. This shift in society from family to school has been going on for some time and thus, when John Patten talked shortly after his inception as Secretary of State for Education (1992) of teachers becoming surrogate parents, he was not suggesting anything new. They have been expected to be that for some time. The White Paper, however, imposes this responsibility as mandated duty, so that the parent as a customer seems to have considerable power with little emphasis on responsibility.

In fact, parents do expect a great deal from schools, not because they are worse parents necessarily, but because they are often more aware of the importance of parenting. The greater awareness of modern psychology with its stress on the importance of childhood puts more pressure on parents to provide the best for their children, yet their lives are just as pressured, though differently pressured, as adult lives have ever been, and schools are seen to be a compensatory and ancillary arm in that parenting. More is expected of schools both academically and pastorally. Of course, many parents recognize this and are openly grateful and collaborative and will also respond willingly to requests from the school for support, be that in relation to the child's progress or in a more altruistic matter. Given the nature of modern society it is not surprising that such expectations have grown or that schools have responded, becoming much more sensitive and supportive institutions for children and parents. In fact, many excellent state schools now provide academic and pastoral care second to none and this is reflected in their general standing in their communities.

A retreat into nostalgia and the measurable

The question for parents in discerning the 'X' factor in a good school is whether they allow themselves to be misled by nostalgic signals in choosing a school and thus sell themselves short. The question equally for schools is whether in attempting to pander to parents' need for security, they, too, distort the school's values, thereby selling themselves and the young people short. Without an open examination of what constitutes a good school, a cautious and conservative mean can easily be encouraged. There is a difficult task for heads of schools to integrate the need for traditional forms and signals of schooling with forward-looking processes. There is a need, too, even in more selective schools, to reconcile the particularized concerns of parents for their own child to the inevitable mix and variety of needs and abilities of all the children in that establishment. Schools also have to reconcile the inevitable demand for vital life-chances in the form of examination results, for example, to broader educational concerns, which are often difficult to express, but have a bearing on the child as s/he prepares for adult life.

Thus the head has to juggle all manner of needs and demands, both the particular and the general. The more catholic the institution, the more varied are those needs and demands. Within this catholic context also it is the nostalgic language of the past which springs more readily to many parents' minds and tongues than the language of the future, and the language of particularity more easily than the universal. For example, parents who want traditional reports based on test scores and a child's place in the class are no doubt reflecting an expectation from their own school days. They may not be aware of the various arguments which now surround such simplicity. A test score, for example, is easy to effect but the implications of such a report on the child or other children less easy to ensure or calculate. It may not be a statement of true ability but a label to which the child then conforms. Some will be spurred on by such measurement and others will be utterly discouraged. In the light of this another parent might prefer a report which focused less on measurement and more on what the child has achieved in general terms. Parents need to be aware of these arguments and the school must find ways to satisfy the various demands and perceptions.

Certainly I, with other heads, have been faced with this sort of dilemma, as I indicated in Chapter 4, where one parent wanted, for example, 'factual' measurement and the other less normative assessment and more 'can do' statements for a child who was dyslexic. Historically, reports have been normative whereas Records of Achievement, the profiles which have in schools increasingly replaced traditional reports, try to incorporate more sophisticated angles on performance, including the child's own perceptions as to how s/he is doing in relation to specific targets. It could be said to be more structured and to say more about expectation and performance than a straight mark does, but a number is more reassuring to some parents. They may well find such scores more readily digestible than a more complex statement but this is not to say that they cannot be educated into broader and more profoundly satisfying records of progress. Indeed, most parents are likely to welcome more sophisticated approaches, recognizing that a sole emphasis on measured outcomes masks the child as a person just as purely open statements deny a degree of rigour and a clear idea of where the child stands in relation to what is expected. The fact is parents want both: the paradox in fact of the 'X amalgam'.

Children not cyphers

We are today more comfortable with things we can measure. At the same time we are a more humane age than ever before. The combination often leads us to embrace impersonal or abstract systems rather than listening and attending to people as Michael Polanyi explains in 'On the modern mind' (1965, pp 12-19):

> ... the modern mind distrusts intangible things and looks behind them for tangible matters on which it relies for understanding the world. We are a tough-minded generation ... in spite of our tough theories [however] our society is more humane than any that existed before ... All our moral fervour which scientific scepticism has released from religious control and rendered harmless by discrediting its ideals, returns to imbue an a-moral authenticity with intense moral approval.

In the opinion of many professionals, the greater weighting given in the National Curriculum to traditional methods and assessment lays a greater emphasis on *measuring* performance than on *developing* people, and schools which wish to incorporate the formative with the apparently definitive will have to find ways of dealing with both expectations and approaches. Though most parents will be familiar with reports which emphasize mainly test scores, those who have experienced more rounded reporting methods will not for the most part wish to return to the unadorned and bald number/grade of the past. How far schools attempt to incorporate both forms of assessment depends very much on the value-underpinning of the school, which either sees children as whole persons or not. It depends, too, on the values of parents and how those values are answered by the process and format of reports/records. Many parents and schools which have already experienced the positives of the Record of Achievement, as opposed to a traditional school report, will want to adapt the aspects of both into one. The Record of Achievement allows the pupil's voice to come through in the form of an element of self-assessment. It also suggests targets in relation to course and competency outlines. The Record's summary document is the culmination of a dialogue with the pupil and with the parent about how learning is proceeding: it is very particular to the pupil and allows parents to enter into the ambiguities of the learning process.

Formative self-assessments are particularly useful in bringing out the person behind the face that we are teaching. For example, when an 11-year-old, in reply to the question in a subject report , 'What help do you now need?' replies, 'I need help with working in small groups for I tend to dominate', or in a quick class self-assessment with a new group another child writes of her French, 'I still find the tenses difficult and I hope you won't get impatient with me', then that child is seen as a person not a cypher and a constructive relationship is much more likely.

It is probably true that schools which make every effort to deal with the individuality of children are the ones which parents favour above all, provided they feel at the same time that their children are receiving a structured curriculum within which they are appropriately stretched. Thus it is in the interest of the children for schools to continue to explore the personalizing of schools. It is also in the interest of education and our culture as a whole, for anonymizing processes produce unhappy and damaged people and it is these people who are building the society of tomorrow. The current emphasis on more traditional methods of measurability at all costs carries a good deal of insensitivity to children and to the notion of an inclusive culture. Such an approach must not be allowed to overtake the strides state education has made not only in becoming a more humane service but one that has increasingly recognized that Gradgrind methods are counter-productive. The reading of Dickens's *Hard Times* should be a constitutional obligation – part of an adult reading list! In suggesting this to one parent concerned to measure his daughter to the nth degree, he replied, 'I have no time for such things: I deal in facts, facts, facts.' I am most relieved to say that he does seem to be in a minority.

A schooling for conformity?

The task for school management in the 1990s has to be to combat this tendency in modern culture to seek reassurance only in the measurable and traditional, for anything which can be measured is usually of the least value and the traditional usually constitutes, with apologies to T.S. Eliot, the words we have for those things we no longer wish to say. There is a similar tension in the greater requirement of teachers that they should become surrogate parents, responsible for 'the spiritual, moral and cultural' development of young people. Increasingly parents look to the schools to provide some moral certainty in a society where traditional forms of authority and belief are rapidly breaking down. The 'back to basics' lobby of the curriculum and school organization is paralleled by a 'back to traditional values' dimension which will also in the terms of the 'X' factor structure the child and let him or her know what it is s/he is expected to do.

In this respect, a head of an increasingly popular school declared to me that what he was after, and what he thought 'his' parents wanted, was 'social conformity with intellectual non-conformity'. When asked whether he did not see a paradox in this, he did not, and yet it is hard to imagine how conformity in one area can be so completely divorced from another. At all events it does behove us to remember that although we may want children to behave in particular ways, the democratic sense and self-reliance which we would deem essential for adult life will only develop where young people are given some room for manoeuvre, however uncomfortable that might be for those of us wanting a quiet and tidy life. Historically a bitter price has been paid as a result of schooling for conformity, and intellectual and moral independence have not been the happy result.

Nevertheless, moral teaching is an important issue for our society and it is an area about which, in the face of a more open society with media influence direct into the sitting room, parents feel much anxiety, particularly as many adults today do not have the convictions about certain moral standards that their parents or grandparents might have done. What, of course, we tend to forget in our fear of today's 'loose ends' is the awful inhumanity of some of those convictions, particularly for girls and women who fell short of social expectations.

In trying to understand what parents might want of a school in terms of moral education, David Pascall, Chairman of the National Curriculum Council, gave some insight in his comment in the *Times Educational Supplement* (29 May 1992):

As a parent of three children, I expect their school to have and communicate a clear vision of the moral values which it and society hold to be important. These include trust, fairness, politeness, honesty and consideration for others. I also look to the school to support our family in bringing our children to spiritual maturity. Spiritual growth in this context does not only apply to the development of religious belief but involves encouraging children to appreciate what is right and wrong, to search for the meaning in life and values by which to live. The NCC does have a role to play, but a supporting not a prescriptive one. My aim has been to stimulate debate but responsibility really does lie at local level – with the

Standing Advisory Councils on Religious Education and with governors and teachers for ensuring that schools face up to questions of spiritual and moral development and that religious education is well taught.

The White Paper puts a similar emphasis on moral considerations through a re-endorsement of religious education and the Collective Act of Worship.

The problem with such statements is that they assume a greater moral consensus and less pluralistic society than we currently have. Once again, there is a wish to return to the traditions and conventions of yesteryear. There is clearly much of worth in traditional values, but it is a desperate phenomenon of our multi-faith and increasingly faithless society that there should be such emphasis in the reforms of education on one culture and minority practices. Though there is admittedly some room for acknowledgement of other faiths and creeds in statements on religious education, the very reassertion of a daily Act of Worship of a mainly Christian nature in schools, which parents and children have to opt out of rather than opt into, does beg considerable questions of:

(a) the place of religious *observance* in a school context; and
(b) our real sensitivity as a society to the multi-cultural dimensions of modern culture.

In many schools the 1944 Act's requirement for a daily Act of Worship has been honoured more in the breach than the observance for the simple reason that schools have grown too large for daily assemblies but, more than that, the social climate and religious observance of families have changed.

There is nevertheless a nostalgia for a world which seems in retrospect more secure and unified. It is often in this spirit that many parents, though they might not attend church themselves, send their children to Sunday School. Schools are similarly expected to prop up forms of reassuring moral influence in the hope that something may rub off without those forms having necessarily any root in the child's own personal and social experience. In the assumption of the required Act of Worship that schools are an arm of the church as identified with state, children are put through a process rather than being part of that process; their questions are submerged in an implicit paternalism which says this is *the case* rather than this is *the question*. The addressing of questions in religious *education*, as distinct from *worship*, is, of course, an entirely different matter and a wholly necessary and desirable thing for schools to do.

Values as underpinning

The fact is there is no moral consensus and convention based on a publicly recognized religion which can be unproblematically invoked for all children: it is like trying to put a cork back in a bottle which for a significant number of people is now devoid of its content. It is not a lack of concern to instil a sense of values and meaning that is at question, it is finding the appropriate forms to do it. Certainly these forms should allow young people to explore questions rather than attempt to give unequivocal answers and individual parents need to tolerate the different viewpoints of others. Parents are not a uniform body in this respect though they are referred to as such.

It is, in fact, the school's whole approach in the overt and hidden curriculum which conveys the real message of values and the 'how' of what is taught and done is as important as the 'what'. In my own school the Personal, Social, Vocational and Moral Education Programme – PSVME – represents a value-underpinning to the curriculum and running of the school rather than a bolted-on extra to a very full timetable. The curriculum planning and method take account of these values which are practised through the teaching and learning. There is, of course, a content but more important than this is the way that content within the existing curriculum is taught.

The emphasis in PSVME is qualitative and seeks to inform our lower and higher aims and objectives:

1. Each individual is worthy of care and respect.
2. Inner growth, though invisible, is as necessary/real as material, intellectual or physical growth.
3. The individual has a responsibility for him/herself and for others.
4. The individual has a responsibility for the future of the world and thus for the immediate environment.
5. Each individual is potentially a fully actualized person to be respected.

6. The aims of PSVME are to enable self-actualization and empowerment to take place as a multi-dimensional experience in a curriculum context which takes account of material, vocational, spiritual, intellectual, physical and political experience and learning.

If pupils are to grow into their truly fulfilled selves with a meaningful sense of values there must be an openly caring and thinking environment in the school where open-minded and honest enquiry pervade a holistic educational experience which works towards points 1-6 above. A PSVME programme will therefore engage pupils in the following emphases:

(a) knowledge of beliefs and values within a questioning framework.
(b) the ability to reason critically, to be able to know the difference between 'I know', 'I feel', 'I think', etc.
(c) the development of empathy and socially interactive skills.
(d) the development of self-awareness, self-regulation and self-reliance.
(e) the practice of cooperation and democracy.
(f) the practice of responsibility to oneself and others.
(g) the practice of enterprise and initiative.
(h) the awakening of moral awareness and tolerance.
(i) the practice of stillness, inner strength and personal character.
(j) the practice of moral courage and strengthening of character.
(k) the notion of building on success and strength and tackling fallibility as a spur to growth and improvement.
(l) competition as competition against oneself (this does not rule out team sport!).

Clearly there is some very particular vocabulary here and this PSVME statement of values was designed initially for internal rather than public discussion, where it needs to be more demystified and less 'high falutin'' perhaps.

Nevertheless, it has been discussed in part as it stands with mixed groups, including parents, where the 'unpacking' has been a necessary part of the process. In other words a statement of values or aims is only a starting point for further understanding of a choice of words: it is the process which is formative not the product. One head related that his proudest achievement after two years spent on a values statement for his school was the establishing of curriculum principles for subject departments to measure their planning by. It was his proudest achievement for it had been accomplished without his help: the values fabric had been thoroughly established by the formative process of the value statement – a process which needs the input of staff, parents, governors and pupils.

This sort of underpinning is difficult to organize and monitor: content and approaches have to be mapped and coordinated by designated staff and be subject to regular monitoring and evaluation if the value statement is to succeed. Its central place in the School Development Plan is essential where it represents a coherence for what all the various subjects and activities are trying to achieve.

Topics and approaches are explored with parents at various open evenings such as one organized by staff and pupils on moral education. Elements from lessons were played out to show parents how issues were tackled and discussed and this was then discussed by the parents. An item on sex education brought forth different parent viewpoints about the wisdom of how much should be covered and at what age. The important part of such evenings is that parents listen to each other as quite divergent views emerge. Such an experience breeds far more insight into other ways of seeing what children can do and understand than would be the case if parents were listening purely to professionals and, indeed, at the end of the evening, when asked whether they felt as parents that the pupils were getting a sound and worthwhile approach, there was, despite an earlier divergence of viewpoint, consensus for us to continue in the same vein.

What particularly impresses parents in such situations is having the young people themselves present for some or all of the time: their maturity and common sense are always warming and bring home to parents a scope of self awareness which they had not perhaps expected. This in itself endorses the school practice and is enjoyable for parents to see and hear. The turnout for curricular discussion evenings varies – sometimes large, sometimes small – but the cumulative awareness and the build-up of parental tolerance and trust through their sharing questions with pupils and each other is significant. Pupils again become more than cyphers or helpless beings to be directed; they are seen rather as persons in their own right, capable of searching for answers and meanings for themselves, provided teaching and learning approaches and the curriculum structure have been thought through accordingly.

A need for balance

There is, therefore, in 'amalgam X' a curious mix which demands tradition – a sense of absolutes, old fashioned rigour, measurability and formal structure – together with something more appropriate to society's needs today which is still structured and disciplined but is more tender, personal, humane and tolerant. The reforms reflect this confusion by emphasizing above all the more tangible elements of the confusion: the traditional forms of control and discipline of the learning process and the 'harder' language of business, competition and technology. The fact of young people as tender plants, their potential wholeness as persons with a capacity for joy and play and the ambiguities of modern culture are left out. Much of the emphasis in the reforms is built on nostalgic memories of the public and grammar schools. These projections, however, do not necessarily reflect the culture of such schools today but in many respects caricature it. In the private sector much has changed over the last years, as the independent head again explained.

The notion, he said, of independent schools being 'rough and tough' academically was not a policy he cared to pursue, that the emphasis increasingly was on more sensitive pastoral care and such broader cultural concerns as Music and the Arts. We shall have to be careful that the National Curriculum does not squeeze out these antidotes to a mechanistic culture, which, as one state school head put it, are the modern spiritual dimension:

> I feel very passionately about the power and force of the expressive arts ... I have learnt so much from seeing good dance teachers work. A young teacher once said to me many years ago that it is not just a bit of brain that comes, it is a whole person – the feelings, the body, the history they have left behind. And therefore enabling children to use their bodies, to enjoy sharing in the context of sound and harmony and colour and feeling – it is a theory of mine that it is the modern-day spiritual dimension. In the last century they would have learnt from the Authorized Version, and so on.

Certainly the Arts figure strongly in our own value curriculum and have had a major impact on our equal opportunities programme, not least in boys doing dance. I am continually struck by the pupils' ability to articulate what the Arts mean to them. In our policy, for example of integrating pupils with a physical disability, one young lady, an accident victim who is confined to a wheel-chair for most of the time, does dance, working through floor exercises. When asked what dance meant to her she replied that it had brought her happiness; it had not only strengthened her muscles but her will-power and she felt it made people see her for *who* she is rather than what she does.

The White Paper reflects the ambiguities of modern culture. It seeks, for example, a return to religious and moral principles but at the same time exposes schools and therefore children, to the rigours of the 'a-moral authenticity' of measurable systems and the market. These ambiguities have not been invented by Government reforms but are factors in a modern society which seeks stability in a rapidly changing world, a world increasingly dominated, through our neglect of ethical voice, by abstract systems and ideologies rather than individuals and corporate purposes. How far schools with their communities can achieve a balance of humane and rigorous systems depends on effective means both to share value questions with school stakeholders and to demonstrate those values in workable strategies. Schools must enable parents to gain a real window on these values in action and to experience the happiness and stability of children in an active and thoughtful curriculum based on pupil involvement, voice and the whole person as part of an inclusive culture; only then will the 'X' factor find flesh and life.

A more deliberate focus on children and on values in action in learning and teaching must help schools to shape *with* their communities the best of the reforms and mitigate the worst. In eradicating and jettisoning the worst, educating parents' judgement of quality through the medium of their children's experience is crucial. As the determinants of what constitutes a good school and as seekers of the 'X' factor, the curriculum needs their watchdog support if it is to remain a National Curriculum for the children, rather than a vehicle for ideological theory or whim.

Chapter 9

Governors and the Appointment of Head

A pivotal appointment

The appointment of a head who, as we have seen is pivotal to the relations, team-building and values of a school, is the single most important responsibility that governors exercise. The head's values need to be sufficiently congruent with those of the governing body but also sufficiently independent to bring in new and fresh ideas and perspectives which any organization needs if it is to stay alive to and fit for all eventualities. Such an appointment in the past required a greater involvement of the LEA Chief Education Officer or his or her representative. Though this involvement is still strong in many areas, there is no longer a requirement on the governing body to involve the LEA in the case of a locally managed school, and certainly not at all for a GMS school. The governing body now has full powers of 'hire or fire', though the wise body will be open to professional advice if it is offered.

Where there is a tradition of apparently congruent values – I say apparently, for sometimes congruence might be a euphemism for complacency – it is always tempting for a governing body to look for the same sort of person in a head as they are used to, with an expression of values that they are used to also. However, though the governors may wish for some continuity in terms of personality and values, the world outside the school does not stand still. It is not that values are likely to change dramatically with a new head, but the style of delivering those values may need to be radically different and take account of a changing world and context.

Grit in the oyster

Institutions can become ossified or too cosy to deal with change or may simply become too slow to recognize it before its implications are upon them. So any institution needs some 'grit in its oyster', that is, some critical self-appraisal, if it is to remain flexible and ready for intelligent · and informed adaptation to changes that might impact upon it, or that it perceives a necessity to implement. Such reaction and proaction will not be value-free and the organization has to set any change against values which have been cherished to date. Being self-aware, therefore, as an institution is essential if new slants and responses to values are to emerge and to be planned for with as much informed assent of stakeholders as possible.

The fact of change in society as a whole makes it impossible for schools to stand outside the arena of that change, and yet some may still try to do this, as the reference to 'oasis' headship indicated in Chapter 2. In the past, where the power base was more clearly that of LEAs and the schools, it was easier for schools to impose the values which they considered in the best interests of the children. Parents wanting to escape from such schools had no option under the catchment system but to send their child to the local school or move house to avoid doing so. Now it is not only a matter of value-congruence within the school, there also has to be some alignment of those values and ways of doing things with the community or communities outside the school. Parents under open enrolment are more likely to try to vote with their feet – the 'exit' strategy referred to in previous chapters.

The head in Chapter 2 who saw heads in terms of 'horses for courses', where they tended to choose schools which reflected their values, was seeing in the situation of a school a *value-given* rather than an opportunity for continual value evaluation and revision in the light of circumstances. This is not to say that principles in themselves can be continually corrupted and changed, but the way they are applied, articulated and understood, and by whom, may have to be constantly renegotiated. Thus any suggestion of too fixed a value-congruence denotes a fixity perhaps not so much of ideas as strategies to deal with those ideas. Value-congruence, therefore, within an institution will be no guarantee of that institution's survival unless those values can be negotiated successfully with the external customers and potentially prospective partners of the organization, namely pupils and parents: pupils because they today often do hold considerable sway in a choice of schools, with parents not wanting to fly in the face of their feelings, and parents, of course, in their mandated power of choice under the reforms.

Gaining some perspective

Governors, therefore, not only need to be able to stand back from their schools themselves in deciding what sort of new perspectives might be required, but they need to be able to discern the prospective head as a professional with, on the one hand, clearly articulated values and aspirations for the school and, on the other, the skills to realize those values in the context of an ever-changing world and more enfranchised public. S/he, therefore, needs to demonstrate more than pure principle; s/he needs to be a strategist with skills in public relations.

Not all schools have equally attractive recruitment possibilities. No incentives are offered nationally for heads to take on more challenging schools. So governors may wish to think of some statement of incentive, but perhaps more important than this, some statement to inspire applicants to meet the challenge defined. So often there is an anxiety to hide any disadvantage and governors might want to consider making the school's particular problems a professional challenge which is recognized rather than fudged.

As we have seen, the head's personal values do play a part in which schools s/he applies for: it has to be, however, a commitment of heart and head. Without heart the applicant will not necessarily apply and without head – ie management overview and competence – heart will not be enough. Such a combination of heart and head was exemplified in the case of one school in the survey, where the head had had to take over as acting head (to become later the appointed head), when HMI panned the majority of subject departments and management practice in the school. Though young and inexperienced, the head felt compelled to take the place by the scruff, as it were, and in a few years had made a remarkable difference. No amount of management science could have produced her commitment, which was fortunately harnessed to considerable competence. The chair explained:

> I share [the head's] dream, that this can be a great school. We are living down a history of bad management, if you like, or, shall we say, maybe not quite so much bad management but mismanagement, inasmuch as people were left to do what they wanted to do; nobody seemed to care. And so when [the new head] came in it was like a breath of fresh air, because here was somebody who wanted to get things done, who had a vision of the school and could see it going places. And, as I say, with her it *is* going ... I would trust her in anything. She is a rare woman, really, these days, because everything she does is for the school. There is very little in it for [her], except hard work, sleepless nights and worry.

In fact, of course there was a great deal in it for this head beyond worry: she was a professional and it was an important professional challenge from which she has now moved on to another headship. The chair is right to find such commitment exceptional but it is there if it can be attracted and harnessed, particularly in a young and energetic head.

Governors need to think, therefore, about the values, aims and real challenges of their establishments and the personal qualities needed to meet them. The advertisement and details must elicit vision, excitement and energy if suitable candidates are to come forward. Governors also need to bear in mind that they are making a considerable investment in a new head, and, therefore, depending on the circumstances, some relocation or incentive plan may be in order. Incentives do not always have to be wholly in the form of salary levels; incentives can also emerge from the recognition by governors of the task which faces the recruit and their declared support for certain measures which might have to be taken. If schools face recruitment problems generally, then vision and a declaration of values are as important and essential as attractive incentive packages.

Chairs of governors interviewed showed evidence of both nervousness and complacency with regard to this considerable responsibility. One governor foresaw great difficulties in gauging someone suitable and commensurate to the task:

> sw: How far are governors in shape ... to actually appoint the right sort of person? Will they want someone with strong convictions which they can identify with? Where will they get their yardsticks?

Now, at [this school] you have your yardsticks worked out to some extent by having been through aims, principles and ethos ... So if [the head] were to go and you were to re-appoint, presumably you would have a yardstick against which you would be measuring?

GOVERNOR: That is true, you are absolutely right in everything you say, but it would be ever so difficult to do it. I hope that doesn't happen because it would be extraordinarily difficult, I think, especially if you were actually promoting somebody to that position rather than asking them to make a sideways move. They would be an unknown quantity. You literally do not know how people will respond to that set of opportunities until they do it, and then of course it may well be too late. We have probably both seen situations in which people who are really excellent seconds-in-command do not really take over and handle the principal task at all well. They are much more at home in a support role than they are in taking the key position. It is a scenario which I find rather discouraging to think about actually ... Having said that, the other thing which is on the agenda for the governing body is to look more closely at these processes of appointing, because we were rather boxed in. What we want to know is, what is the limit of the equal opportunities framework, and which bits do we have discretion over? ... But that is largely because we have a range of people, many of whom come from private industry where they would never have dreamed of having to follow the plans that we had to, in terms of making sure everybody was asked the same question, and in the same order, and all the rest of it ...

'It's as simple as that'

This governor, then, was not only daunted at having to discern the qualities of a good head but showed some concern, too, about prevailing advice on how to conduct interviews in general. Such advice often comes from the LEA and governors are sensibly wary of stepping outside any personnel advice because, of course, they either are not themselves wholly versed in educational personnel matters or may not even have experience of them from industry. Clearly, however, governors are beginning to question that advice and are thinking more widely than the orthodoxy to date.

Other governors, by contrast, had no qualms at all about the responsibility and felt that they would tackle the problem quite capably as and when the occasion arose: the process seemed to be quite simple:

CHAIR: I would want to get the wording of the advertisement such that I would be looking for a whole person to educate whole people. It's as simple as that. That is basically the ethos. That is the sort of person we have always employed – we've hit bullseye or jackpot every time.

However, the head today is more than an educator, though s/he is still that, s/he is the interface and pivot in the organization of a whole host of relationships, teams and networks. That in today's changing circumstances the role and function of the head is still not clear was evident in a discussion with a head and his chair:

CHAIR: You are absolutely right. The interesting point you raised is the changing demands that are going to be made upon a head of a school. One almost wonders if you don't really require of a headteacher any teaching qualifications at all! I wonder if one day some school will take it upon itself to appoint what, for want of a better word, might be described as a manager ... A person who would be a tough nut, who would be a professional manager who would be able to deal with the unseen enemy [a governor described]. In the engineering companies with which I am familiar, you don't need an engineer at the top, you need someone who is prepared and worldy-wise ... however good a headteacher is at teaching ... some governors might regard that as a bit of an indulgence ... the new breed of head will do less and less teaching, I think, and more management ... how to relate to governors, and how to be aware of the political scene, that you described so nicely.

HEAD: There is a little bit of an alarm bell ringing with me there. I don't teach a lot ... But I worry about losing touch with the children, and the possibility of making decisions which are not entirely relevant, which are not entirely realistic, because I have lost touch with the grass roots ... At the end of the day I live or die as a head by · standards that the children achieve academically and in sports and drama and music and all the rest of it ... what I am about most of the time is lifting the aspirations of the children and lifting standards.

CHAIR: Here ... the budget is, say, two million pounds in rounded terms ... it is a fair-sized little company that would have as its chief executive a guy who would be experienced in management of people

... of money. He becomes something of a legal guide. He would be knowledgeable politically, and all the other things a head has to be ... the experience a head acquires through teaching may not be the best experience to equip him to deal with all these different tasks that a head has to confront in a new society.

HEAD: You don't achieve a headship these days normally without pretty hefty management courses. I have been on a lot of them, not all terribly good. But I am still worried about the possibility of getting out of touch with what we are really about.

The head drives the ship

What both head and chair are demonstrating is the multi-dimensional role of headship today and the expectations upon it. Whether teaching regular classes is essential to keeping in touch with children and standards is debatable. Seeing the head as purely a manager can be equally simplistic: it depends what is meant by the term 'manager' for the head has to have a deep cultural understanding of his or her school and the social, political and economic conditions of that culture.

Many governors, confident in having in their head quality leadership, feel able to adopt a policy of intervention by exception. This was the predominant stance of most governors interviewed. If the head is coping there is no need to interfere with professional scope and compass, to the extent in one case that all personnel matters of recruitment were devolved to the head to get on with. In the case of private schools, too, it was clear that once the governors had appointed the head s/he was expected to get on and run the school with minimum interference. This point emerged with particular reference to a developing Arts policy at the school due to the leadership of the head:

SW: Where does that change come from, to widen the curriculum? Do you think parents themselves are demanding that now of private schools, or is it proactive on [the school's] part, saying to parents that this is important?

CHAIR: I know there was some parental pressure, but equally I think the governors appoint the headmaster hopefully for what he is. They look at his track record, they interview him at length, and they appoint him for the areas where they think he is going to score. Then, even in the independent sector, the headmaster is left to drive the ship.

sw: So the head's philosophy and ... values, once the governors have heard what he has to say, or ... she has to say, ... they are very much encouraged to get on with it, and providing they are successful then the governors feel pretty confident.

CHAIR: Yes, one is very aware that in the independent sector at the moment there is considerable pressure on, shall we say, the business success of the schools; the pressure is on, for boarding especially ... some pretty far-reaching decisions have had to be made on boarding, and why have some schools gone co-ed? Is it for the best of reasons or is it purely to get the funding up? There are schools under pressure, and headmasters' heads are rolling now at a greater rate than ever before.

Governors still have a role to play, this chair continued, in supporting the head's 'vision' with all sorts of areas of expertise being necessary in the governing body such as accountancy, law and building expertise:

CHAIR: One implants that and makes sure all those areas are covered within the governing board. If not, you've got problems, I suspect. But the headmaster can be guided, and is guided, by the governing board, by his senior masters and mistresses, and I dare say, by his wife and family and what is going on around him.

A more vulnerable position

There is obviously an optimum amount of non-intervention and intervention by a governing body: too much or too little not only may cause problems for the head but may well affect, too, the competence of the governing body in due course. Standing back too far from the issues and dilemmas is just as bad as meddling in management rather than governance issues. One chair, looking back on the induction of a head, could see with hindsight that she had been very much left to it in a difficult situation of change. Not all governors agreed with the changes and some doubted her methods of discipline. This doubt was communicated to her in niggling and unhelpful ways rather than ever as the subject of open and honest debate. She herself could look back and see that her methods had been rather impatient and single-minded and she felt perhaps she had ruffled feathers more than she needed to have done. Such situations are not unusual, for sometimes change is needed but not sought by existing staff; governors, too, can be unwilling to rethink.

It is also the case in today's situation that heads who try to shoulder all decisions alone are putting themselves into a self-punishing and very vulnerable position. Some non-intervention by governors has more to do with a complacent selfishness and abdication than it ever has to do with giving the head room for manoeuvre. Several chairs, for example, did concern themselves with pastoral care of the heads, watching that they did not overdo things and ensuring they took enough rest. Of course, such a stance depends on the relationship between the chair and head and on the trust built up, for there is a delicate balance between friendly care and paternalism. Nevertheless, new and inexperienced heads do need some consideration from governing bodies about how things are going together with some room for manoeuvre: heads certainly do not need neglect.

A balance of heart and head

It will never be possible to eradicate tensions entirely, nor necessarily desirable, but an audit of the school's management needs before appointment would go some way to drawing a context together for open debate so that when the head goes into action, the tensions are already out in the open. Ideally some outside view is helpful, though governors who will be ultimately responsible for the audit and appointment should try to make up their own minds rather than have them made up for them. If relations with the LEA are good it could be a representative of the Chief Education Officer, or other consultancy agencies, including the new inspector teams and higher education researchers. Internal review and opinion should be considered, involving parents, staff, pupils and teachers. Certainly governors should try to gain as much perspective as possible and be aware that the familiar is always seductive and the known an inhibition as well as a support. Like any family, members of a school cannot always see what is obvious to more detached observers; equally, detached observers cannot always judge the heart and 'hidden glue' of such a group.

Of course, bringing in an informed but detached view is likely to be an expense to the school but the appointment of a head is a major investment and should not be something which governors become too penny-pinching about. The wrong decision could cost them very dear indeed. For this reason it has become more usual for headship interviews to span at least two days, often three. These days are not necessarily consecutive and may involve candidates in a variety of tasks and challenges to do with school organization and budgets. They may, too, involve contact with a variety of stakeholders, including pupils, but above all they should include exploration of the candidates' values and philosophy and conscious strategies to implement that philosophy.

A track record of actual proaction is something that should also be looked for in previous posts, for rhetoric at interview is difficult to test. The outgoing head may be able to advise on such procedures but it really is a question for the governing body to sort out for themselves: a task which can tax professionals in education, so not an easy one for any governing body with a preponderance of lay people.

No absolute blue-print but a clarification of values

There is no absolute blue-print and governors will need to think very carefully and perhaps take good advice before ultimately making up their own style and format of advertisement, recruitment details for candidates and interview procedure. Certainly, however, the audit and review will clarify or reassert values and directions for the future which should in turn inform the details to candidates and the process of the interview itself. An advertisement having been placed and applications received, criteria for selection can be drawn up which will be informed by the values and policies already explored.

Again here governors might wish to seek advice from professionals but have to make up their own minds as to whether they act upon it. Having made an appointment, the clarification of values, aims and objectives can continue with a succinct press release immediately following the appointment with some statement of confidence in the candidate expressed, to be followed by a more detailed interview of the successful candidate by a local reporter where some indication of the profile and values of the new head will provide him or her with the beginnings of a platform for the future. Where heads are new to an area such contact can be made by the governing body, who will thereby introduce the head to the local press in a positive way.

The process, therefore, would be in following sequence, ensuring that as many people as possible feel part of the event:

- Internal audit and review of values/policies
- Consideration of external view/consultancy
- Formulation of post details and candidate qualities

- Planning interview procedures and participants
- Announcement of appointment to school community
- Press release prior to press interview of new head
- Press profile of head and some comment on direction of plans

Undoubtedly, where there has been a history of partnership and optimum involvement in the values issues and strategies of the school, governors will be in a stronger and more time-efficient position to make judgements, both about interview procedures and of suitable candidates. The fact is that many state school governors are still very new to their responsibilities and are nervous and inexperienced in many areas. Breadth of knowledge and expertise need to be built up, not in theory in valuable committee work, but through acquaintance of actual instances of school life.

By taking part in staff recruitment interviews with the head and other staff, considerable understanding is built up of all manner of things to do with the school. Informal involvement, too, in pupil discipline and pastoral care not only provides a longer road before formal measures of exclusion are taken but introduces governors to everyday problems and to parents and pupils as sympathetic persons endeavouring with the staff to counsel the child on to the right road. Team-building exercises are important both for governors as a body and in sessions with parents, pupils and staff where discussions of values and policy issues, rather than management nuts and bolts only, clarify the context of the school to governors, often busy people in their own fields. Ensuring, too, a balance of people and competences on the governing body is an added help.

Mutual support

It behoves all heads, for the sake of quality recruitment, to build up consciously the awareness and competences of governors to enable them to gain quickly and usefully the sophistication needed for any eventuality, including the most important of all, the appointment of a new head. Many heads do feel threatened by the apparent power of governors under new legislation, or view the inducting and constant briefing of governors as an additional and stressful burden. With membership turning over every four years as governor terms come to an end, it is indeed a never-ending task. Nevertheless, if heads do not see and respond to governors as a key team of the school, not only will they lose out on the support that might be given, but they are likely to exacerbate the situation of either wholly dependent governors who can become apathetic or over-confident governors who bravely go where angels fear to tread. Heads are, therefore, also responsible with governors for the quality of the heads who will be appointed in the future. The continuing calibre of the profession is to a great extent still in professionals' hands even though governors appoint.

It is the case, too, that governors need to consider the induction and continuing support of the head, though they themselves may be following a steep learning curve. The clarification of aims and values prior to appointment and discussions at the actual appointment must be shared by the whole governing body so that potential differences of views can come out in the open. The head equally as part of his or her interview and induction, needs to clarify his or her values and strategies: s/he may find that not all governors will agree but ideas cogently argued tend to command respect. Heads and governors need to work to help each other; not all governing bodies will be able to rely on an experienced head for advice and not all heads will be able count on governing bodies being confident and unified teams. Nevertheless the roles are interdependent and this interdependency has to be recognized as the paradox of the powers and values which are now devolved to schools.

Chapter 10

The Market Place and School Communities

The Great Escape

The emergence of the common school – the comprehensive school – put schools at the centre of their communities, defined by historical, geographical and socio-economic factors. Until the advent of open enrolment, there was no escape for parents and children from such catchment definition except by moving house. Now open enrolment is being further developed to incorporate a supermarket system, where a diversity of schools, of different types and character, is offered to parental choice. This was certainly the expectation of the Government's White Paper, 1992. Instead of schools responding to particular and defined communities, the notion exists of schools defining themselves, irrespective of their immediate community, as representing a particular ethos or niche in the market. Schools may consider, for example, becoming a Magnet School or a Technology School, or having some other self-determining emphasis.

The purpose of such diversity, its advocates would suggest, is not only to foster the sort of academic excellence and specialization which it is felt the old grammar/technical schools system offered, but it is also a way to ensure mobility and escape for those children who find themselves in schools which are perceived to be failing. Thus the Great Debate, instigated by James Callaghan in 1976 in regard to the state system, seems now to be turning that system not directly towards overt selection but to a Great Escape: through open enrolment, the assisted places scheme, GMS, CTCs, Magnet Schools and so on. No grammar school agenda has been overtly stated, perhaps because any suggestion of a return to selection is not likely to meet with public approval. Brian Simon addresses this issue in *Does Education Matter?* (1985, p 219):

> Whatever people may say to public opinion pollsters ... when the matter comes down to earth in an attempt to destroy local systems, comprehensive education, it seems, can call on a really massive degree of support ... attempts in Berkshire and Wiltshire to extend existing selective procedures met with an ... unyielding opposition from local populations, again involving mass meetings and consistent pressure on Tory councillors ... At Redbridge also an overt attempt to turn back the clock and reintroduce (or extend) selective schooling was again met with a public outcry.

The dissatisfaction in some people's minds with what is perceived to be the levelling effect of neighbourhood comprehensives, however, has never gone away, and many see in the reforms an attempt to bring back selection by the back door. Barry Hugill, writing in the *Observer*, 10 May 1992, sees the potential 'creaming off' of specialist schools as creating a new underclass:

> How do we cope [with], let alone educate, the stratum fashionably dubbed 'the underclass'?
>
> A very similar question was posed 30 years ago as the move towards ... comprehensivization began. The three-tier structure introduced by the 1944 Act – grammar, technical, secondary modern – was a disaster. It branded well over half the nation's 11-year-olds as failures and had appalling consequences for the economic development in the Sixties and Seventies. The danger is that the 'specialism' becomes a euphemism for 'selection'. There is a moral egalitarian case against selection, but the economic one is stronger ... Mr Patten's historic task is to develop a strategy to create excellence for all. Re-creating a two- or three-tier system is the lazy option ... If Mr Patten does not act, 'ghettoization' of our schools is inevitable.

Achieving stars

The matter of ghetto schools may indeed be exacerbated by the diversity and specialization envisaged by the White Paper, but the fact that they exist already to a greater or lesser extent cannot be ignored. There have been, and still are, doubts about comprehensive education in its effectiveness in combating the deprivation of inner city areas where the social issues often dominate the agenda, thereby negating chances of any upward mobility. It has been argued that children cannot always rise above their circumstances, whereas at least under the grammar school system children were placed according to ability and there would be the upward pull of motivated children. These problems cannot be underestimated and were highlighted in interviews with heads and governors in the survey. A chair of governors and local Labour county councillor of a well-run inner city school depicted her ambitions for the young people in her charge and her disappointments:

> I represent the area all the children come from, so I feel it is very important for the elected member to serve one's schools ... I think the main concern in this area is that it has had a high level of unemployment for a long period of time ... it is difficult to break down the problems associated with that. Plus, the area has always had a 'name' ... I see the children in the infants' school, families going through, and it worries me at times that I am not seeing many, if any, taking an opportunity to step up ... I don't expect them all to achieve stars, but I want them all to have the opportunity to be able to do so.

Such a reflection would be seized on by those politicians and pundits who perceive a levelling factor in comprehensive education. The notion of schools betraying parents and children has been part of Government thinking for some time. John Major, in a speech to the Adam Smith Institute in June 1992, called for an end to 'a giant left-wing experiment in levelling down', and John Butcher in his address to the RSA (1990, p 611), quoted in Chapter 1, has sympathy with Paul Boateng's argument, outlined in a speech in Oxford, that schools in some inner cities have betrayed the children, particularly those of the ethnic minorities:

> In a very brave speech in Oxford in the summer of 1989 Paul Boateng took this theme up and understandably used the strong word 'betrayal'. He talked of the betrayal of inner city kids: somehow many of the schools in inner cities were not delivering the same product ... [as] the suburban or the rural schools.

The message comes through very clearly: it is not social conditions which cause failure, it is the low expectations and management methods of the schools. Thus the White Paper (1992, p 49):

> Schools must not be allowed to fail their pupils. That requires clear and effective action by governing bodies, local authorities and at national level. Failure is not want of resources. Many schools have a lot of money but produce poor education. The failure is usually one of leadership and of management at school level. It has shown that, with strong leadership and effective management, schools in disadvantaged areas can flourish. The Government applauds the achievements of the headteachers and staffs of these schools; failing schools should learn from them. The key conditions for success in a school are:
>
> - a high level of parental and community support;
> - clear and widely understood objectives;
> - consistently high expectations of pupils; and
> - thorough monitoring and review of performance.
>
> The Government is determined to see these conditions become the norm in schools that are currently failing their pupils.

While, therefore, the reforms do not assert a return to selection, and indeed the Secretary of State for Education has been at pains to make clear that no opted-out school has been granted such selective status yet, there is nevertheless an evident concern to enable escape from those neighbourhoods where schools are defined adversely by socio-economic class or are perceived to be failing.

Escape as intervention

The City Technology College, for example, exemplifies this emphasis on escape in its supra-school and supra-community position. The one visited in the NEAC survey was even situated almost symbolically outside the town. This isolation in fact is likely to be short-lived, for more housing is envisaged on the surrounding fields. Nevertheless, its buildings stood proud in an empty landscape. It seemed like a visiting space-ship or time capsule, acting as a Pied Piper in gathering in children from all over the city. The head clearly saw the CTC as an interventionist opportunity to do something for deprived and disad-vantaged children – something he had felt unable to do in his previous headship in a difficult inner city school. He had had to concede that his previous school seemed to him to be fighting a losing battle, for the school had difficulty in attracting staff:

It was no wonder that the youngsters had social problems ... It was a monumental effort to try to give these kids an education. I felt that the only way that [the experience] had benefited me was really to be able to identify that there were certain specific needs that were required to be invested into inner cities and deprived urban areas in order to make education work.

It was for this reason that this experienced head had chosen to take on a City Technology College where he is determined to ensure a balanced comprehensive intake including, as far as it can be managed, a balance of social and economic class. This he was achieving, he felt, though some primary heads had initially assumed he was only likely to be interested in the ablest and best-behaved. He had seen the CTC experiment as the opportunity to create the ideal conditions for all children and not least the socially deprived. A man of acknowledged social conscience, he nevertheless felt, despite possible accusations that he had been simply seduced by the resources and privileges not enjoyed by many ordinary state schools, that the experiment of the CTC was a more positive alternative for the children he wished to help than his previous school had been:

It wasn't [the lure of the resources] ... it was deprivation and seeing that, really, a lot more was needed than just goodwill in order to solve the difficulty ... The reason I am here is to try to demonstrate that with suitable resources and with a suitably motivated teaching force you can actually overcome the difficulties, and that is what I am here for.

The chair of governors confirmed the same idealism:

We started off with a basic philosophy, which was that produced by the Secretary of State in his pamphlet about CTCs, and we developed it from there. I believe myself that we are the only ones who have held true to that all the way through ... It is quite clear that we have established a reputation both within the business and outside the business for doing what we set out to do ... we appointed a principal who is a first-rate headmaster ... he has a proven record ... his commitment is beyond doubt ... really the big problem in education in my perception is the lack of leadership, that head-teachers unfortunately do not get the training that they need to run these sorts of establishments ... Now, we felt that every child deserves the best possible education. So we set out, and we were quite determined to make sure that we had an all-ability group so that we could demonstrate what can be achieved with lower groups. So we were quite determined ... not to be selective ... What we wanted to do was to make the child the focal point, and to make the teacher a manager ... we wanted to see more activity for the pupil ... it was an opportunity to develop new ideas and new techniques.

The educational laboratory

The CTC above enjoys high parental and pupil commitment as well as the opportunity to introduce from scratch, with keen staff, new ways of working with pupils. Setting up a new building and administrative structure also enables the use of new techniques and administrative gadgetry such as a computerized registering of pupils. It represents almost an educational laboratory, where experiments in new management and curriculum ideas can be tried out in near perfect conditions. The restaurant which was shared by staff and pupils – a deliberate strategy to break down the tendency in schools of a 'them and us' between adults and children – was executive quality and children were very likely to feel themselves valued and special.

The CTC does represent an opportunity to work on innovative curriculum approaches in a wholly new situation without the drag factor of historical expectations and staffing. The CTC is attractive to staff and to parents with its 'high tech' image and modern environment. The focus of the CTC is not defined by tradition or a particular community but by what are perceived to be the educational needs of children. The school defines its aims and objectives in relation to that context proactively, rather than reactively. This lack of rootedness and tradition is, however, a double-edged sword, for there is no resting in an existing community identity or cohesiveness. It was clear from the head's reflections on his school that the CTC's parents were highly interested in, and motivated by, all that went on; no doubt friendships and connections were and are being forged, but such schools have to deal with the lack of positive history and tradition which some state and public schools can draw on in terms of reference points and identity.

This is not to say, of course, that there cannot be double-edged swords in serving more historically and geographically defined communities, as the councillor quoted earlier indicates. Apart from her concern for pupil under-achievement, there was a more general concern in the school at the lack of parent voice and representation. Such a parental vacuum leaves the school vulnerable when it comes to a need for parents to stand up in their support of the school: in the more autonomous position of schools today parental voice and advocacy will need to become the mainstays in safeguarding schools' and communities' best interests.

Empowering communities

The effect of low parental involvement is also to breed a low expectation of such involvement in school staffs and governors, which creates a self-perpetuating vicious circle. If schools give up on such involvement and advocacy, then they can fall into the trap in their attitudes and expectations of working always on *behalf* of their communities in a patronizing and paternalistic way. In the survey there were emergent strategies of deliberate and proactive policies to counter apparent apathy where it existed, such as an investment in a public relations post, professional attention to the messages, covert and overt, of the school, parent 'sounding' groups and greater emphasis on personalized contact. The challenge of strengthening such strategies has to be met in the future if autonomous schools are to help their communities to help themselves. Such strategies have to start with the question of how far are the community's and school's needs aligned. This requires an open examination of school/community values through the process of value-mapping mentioned in Chapter 4. In other words, if management becomes too defined by the community's passivity or silent assent, rather than by a search for shared values and an investment in mechanisms of empowerment, then the expectations of all stakeholders are implicitly lowered.

It is a paradoxical situation, for heads and governors need to define their community in order to refine strategies to meet its needs, but those strategies should not be ones that placate or absorb the community's shortcomings but ones which never cease to challenge and prod the community into recognizing its strengths. It is a fine line between respect and paternalism, as the extract of a conversation with a head working in a deprived inner city area illustrates:

HEAD: It is possible in [a middle-class] environment that some construct of the curriculum or some curriculum principle could be challenged at governor level, at parents' meeting level, in a formal discourse with the head, by a long letter or by arm-wrestling over the table. At [this school] that would find very different forms of expression, but it would still happen. And what you actually depend on there is skilled communicators, who can ... keep the communications going. The route into that [here] is very much at head of year level, where there are some real bedrocks and bastions of the community operating ... [staff] who probably taught the parents who have come to talk to them, and ... they interpret [the concerns] in a professional sense for the rest of the organization ... It was you who put the words in my mouth a few years ago. We were talking of serving the highly defined community of X ... I think the phrase you used is 'first define your community'. I do believe that is the first function of the head, to understand what it is you are dealing with. In our case it is relatively straightforward. Its a modulus, geographically defined; it is socio-economically all of a level ... in a middle-class area ... a different set of professional skills is necessary. It could well be that you need to define [a middle-class] community in a number of different ways according to the context you are working with.

An unresolved tension

A tension arises because the reforms are attempting two things at once. The Government is juggling a meritocratic agenda, where cream is expected to rise to the top, with one where the Government appears to be the recognized social conscience of the nation. The two aims, however, sit together uncomfortably, for as F. Hayek, an exponent of the free market, explains (1978, p 57):

To discover the meaning of what is called 'social justice' has been one of my chief preoccupations for more than ten years. I have failed in this endeavour – or rather, have reached the conclusion that, with reference to a society of free men, the phrase has no meaning whatever.

There is an unresolved paradox therefore between a pull of social engineering through market mobility in the reforms, and the need to demonstrate care for all children, regardless of class or the schools in which they find themselves placed. Thus the White Paper seeks to disassociate school 'failure' from communities and locations by focusing on the difference that good management can make to children's performance. The Government has pledged to deal with 'failing' schools through Education Associations which will go in to improve the school; failing that, the school will be closed. These remedial teams will work under the auspices of the CTC Trust, which is clearly seen as the cutting edge in terms of managerial expertise, and they will represent the Government's belief that it is not communities which define schools but good management that defines good communities.

Only time will tell if these teams prove to be more effective, and there is much understandable scepticism about the suggestion, but this 'holding of the thin red line', as it were, is interesting in a particular respect, namely, that the criteria for judging these schools will rest more heavily on evidence of parental and community involvement than on examination outcomes. There will be consideration, too, of truancy levels. This is a welcome shift and suggests a focus on strategies to involve the stakeholders, which have to be of interest to any head faced with apparent apathy or passivity. It is of interest indeed to anyone concerned for integrative and participative management in schools.

Community solidarity

There is no simple answer to the tension which exists between social mobility and social solidarity, ie 'escape' versus community-based schools, but in the atomized culture of society today there have to be very good reasons for any changes in education which split and weaken communities which to date have been relatively cohesive. The effect of greater autonomy and specialist schools is that children are already having to travel longer distances to school – either to schools of their choice, or because their local school is full. This scenario has already caused a great deal of anguish and controversy in boroughs like Hillingdon and Bromley where there are quite a number of GMS schools deciding their own admissions. Of course such policies are not only divisive for children they are also divisive for the communities of those children. It is supermarket values rather than the community values of working together in some sort of rooted context and relationship.

In this way the problems faced by children in the past, and indeed still faced in some areas, in being hived off to grammar schools or secondary moderns, are being supplemented or replaced by other potentially divisive factors. Though the Government talks of parity of esteem between different types of school, this is no guarantee of harmony. Indeed, a similar phrase was used of the tripartite system, and the move from the local common school to 'specialist' schools will elicit its own price. Instead of being necessarily centres of their local community, schools will be centres of a more widely scattered community. Instead of representing catholic values and aptitudes, schools of the future could become more narrowly focused, with an attendant loss of constructive differences and variety of people.

The potential breaking-up of neighbourhood schools, for all their flaws, needs much greater airing than it has had to date. School communities could become more selectively defined, as diversity/specialism bites into the traditional fabric, but equally, without families having any other connectedness or roots than their child's attendance at the school, there could well be a greater 'thrown-togetherness' in school communities which could be more difficult to manage. In the absence today of institutions which unite communities, in the way formerly the church might have done, school leaders need to weigh carefully any move to specialization, not only in relation to their curriculum, but in terms of how far it is truly worthwhile to break up communities into further fragments. They must weigh, too, the loss to their own establishment of the advantage of community spirit and cohesiveness in terms of support for the school and the managerial implications of working across so many traditional boundaries and local groups and services.

The rural deprivation which Henry Morris sought to combat in his community schools may have a slightly different twist today but his ideas are no less relevant to our increasingly dislocated society. Families moving into an area like my own, for example, can find in the Community College something of a replacement for the extended family they have lost: we have play-groups, a work-place nursery, clubs and societies of various kinds, as well as adult classes and youth clubs scattered through our six main feeder villages. It is clear from the 1991 White Paper that Community Colleges are going to have to change and deal with new regulations and paymasters, but the spirit of community education still rests with communities working together on mutual education and support. Schools in their autonomous position today need that spirit more than ever, as does each member of society. The more scattered and diffuse the identity of the school's community is the more the school will need clearly identifiable values to weld the parts of its community together and to elicit support and loyalty from them. It is just such a model that one chair of governors eloquently described:

> We hold the same criteria for other members of staff that we do for the head. We want people who have vision, who would build on what we already have, and I think what we already have is a caring community, a school that looks forward and never looks back ... We want to serve the community and give them the best school possible ... not just in examination results although these are important, but in the tutorial side of things, the actual caring for the parents themselves ... what [the head] has tried to do through working groups with parents, is to get the school to be aware of what parents think, feel and want, not just what the educationalists think we should be achieving. Also, to be abreast of changes before they are actually forced upon us. I think it is very easy for teachers to say we run an open door philosophy. Unless they are shouting it from the rooftops and meeting parents on a regular basis (parents' evenings, PTA events) the reality can be quite different. But I think the most important thing about a school is that it must belong to everybody. It is not just a place for teachers to work, it is not just a place for students to learn. It should be a whole community. I feel the ethos of this school, one of its strengths, is that it does not have to be 'pulled along'. People feel confident enough to act on their own initiative; we have many gifted people with leadership qualities.

A living entity

Schools are not laboratories or purely centres of specialist excellence, they are living entities and at best living communities. Schools which cut themselves off from a defined community through specialist status could miss a great deal in terms of the texture and coherence which a local community can offer. Schools which are rooted in a community may need on the other hand to consider whether they allow their values and strategies to be too much defined by that community; they must ask themselves whether they are becoming too paternalistic or patronizing or perhaps even defensive.

At all events, for those school leaders more interested in an integrative than disintegrative culture, working with communities, as the chair above outlines, presents the best possibility: it is one that Henry Morris envisaged to combat rural deprivation and it is one which can still combat the loss of society's common purpose at the manageable level of the school. Such a model suggests that relationships and community context are as important as a focus on specialization – indeed it might be said more important. Though there are considerable concerns over the downward pull of certain schools, social mobility has to be balanced with social solidarity and school leaders who believe firmly in the latter will work to maintain their schools as the centres of unfettered initiative which Henry Morris envisaged, providing a bulwark in this age for the refining of community purpose.

Chapter 11
Concluding Thoughts

Supreme individualism

The climate of education today has strong disintegrative forces within it. It reflects a confused culture which is emerging from one order to another; this new order is still formulating itself. This is not a new phenomenon, for every age has its cultural shifts and rebirths. However, in this century, with its pace of technological and social change, the situation is exacerbated by the accelerating loss of traditional conventions and acknowledged sources of authority. As a multi-faith and faithless society we are undergoing almost a second Reformation. There is a similar pattern of rejecting the mediation of paternalistic regimes; however, the individual often does not have a higher authority or purpose on which to call. S/he has to fall back on his or her own values and meanings. It is an age, therefore, of the most supreme individualism, but it is not an individualism which has behind it a common culture and interpretation of the good life, and this means that we do not have a common language of values and meanings.

A faith in mechanisms

This loss of common purpose and shared values in our society encourages a tendency to turn away from the immeasurable areas which are concerned with value or ethics and to substitute for such considerations a reliance on the apparently neutral language of technical and operative mechanisms. Our strong drive to reject authority and our increasing inability to share private values leads us into silent systems such as the market to determine the outcomes of social decisions. Schools as social institutions are not exempt from this trend and thus, here, too, children and their learning have become commodities and anarchic self-interest the governing principle of our lives.

Values examined

The clock cannot be turned back. We shall not submit ourselves to an imposed collectivism, no matter how difficult the free-for-all proves. What we must do, however, is to examine more actively the values that we each hold in our school communities, so that clarity can emerge, and differences of value can be examined within a context where mutual respect and informed contact are built up between the school and its community, and between schools. The reforms in education, though politically driven, do not represent a purely political emphasis in our society. In many respects the political emphasis is itself the logical expression of a society which does not examine fundamental principles and values as they apply to everyday life. We have traded too long on inherited assumptions. If we are surprised that the values we thought were absolute appear no longer to have power, it is because we have neglected ideas as being as important as actions. The time has come where the break-up of traditional structures and assumptions requires voice not silence: schools have this as an educative mission whether they relish the prospect or not. The fact of change will not go away and it is inevitably the responsibility of school leaders to work to establish with colleagues and other stakeholders what values and forms of education need to be conserved or retrieved.

The school as educative centre

Schools as educative centres should be experiment stations for ideas and cooperative processes, not for continual operational and competitive experiment, except where the former is aided by the latter. Ideas and values must drive our organizations and systems, and not the other way round. In the curriculum designed for the children and in our interaction with the public, there needs to be a continual reminder and emphasis on reflective thinking and a sharing of questions and dilemmas. The school in its scale is the obvious place for the reconstruction of value thinking to occur. Schools which suppress such thinking in favour of glib packaging are denying the intrinsic function of a school, which is to encourage critical thinking and the management of human values.

In furthering systems which fragment communities, schools are also delaying the regeneration of community spirit and identity. The tension between social mobility and community solidarity presents questions to which we have no clear solutions at present, but to be aware of the questions is at least a start. Heads need to make time within their development for such thinking and they need to encourage it in every possible form in their school communities.

Focusing communication

Despite the upheaval of change at present, there will never be a better time for any complacency about educational values to be faced. What is needed now may appear as yet another problem to be resolved but it is an essential one: we need more communication and discussion in our school communities, but because of pressure, the pitch and focus of such discussion needs to be clearly targeted. Change is best absorbed by focusing the public on the central importance of education. Though a tense time for many communities, the various debates and learning which is occurring within current changes represent a healthy trend towards a more mature culture, where people have to engage with the realities of ideas applied to institutions which they thought would never change.

Heads need to be alert to the needs of their stakeholders to have their questions and concerns addressed. Thus heads must learn to stand back from the coal-face more often. Where heads have created a climate of value exploration and clarity, it becomes easier to delegate and enlist commitment, and staff become more confident in dealing with developmental as well as operational tasks. The value-narrative of any organization has to be kept going as a continual conversation with, and between, stakeholders. To achieve this heads need to be clear themselves about where they wish to go, and they need to have time also to ensure that such conversations take place.

Unspoken baggage

Governors need to raise their sights, too, away from the minutiae of management to the matters of value and policy. They need to choreograph their meetings to cover the essence of policy, leaving the concrete to working sub-groups. Above all they need to concentrate on building teams which can get on more quickly with issues because they already have the unspoken baggage out of the way. Chairs and heads need to manage the values of their governing bodies and to create opportunities for latent conflicts and consensus to emerge.

A match of value and strategy

A thinking and reflective approach needs to be harnessed to skill at the operational level. The separation of operations from an ethical context has to be eradicated in school management; fixed and rigid ideas which attach to ways of doing things must be replaced by a constant openness of mind which is adaptable without losing sight of value-directions. In the volatile climate of today, leaders need to be quick on their feet while holding to the general value-narrative of their institution: the skilful leader will know there is more than one way to skin a cat, precisely because his or her general value emphasis is quite clear.

The danger of the parochial school

The training of heads and their staffs needs to avoid any possibility of parochialism or pedestrian thinking, which could be an outcome of isolated schools, through development programmes which increasingly involve collaboration between professionals and the public. The thinking school of the future will be quite prepared to promote seminars, conferences, and activities which involve governors, parents, professionals, and in some instances also pupils, in joint training and development.

A Rée of inspiration

Perhaps the central message of this book can best be summarized in a quote from Harry Rée, who in his turn quotes from Henry Morris. Harry Rée was a biographer and life-long friend of Henry Morris, as well as a distinguished educator in his own right. Before he died in 1991 he worked for the Community Education Development Centre at Coventry and edited its monthly newspaper, *Network*. Both Harry and

Henry Morris were and still are influential and eminent educators of a broader public; both were immensely flexible and adaptable thinkers and operators; both demonstrated a vision which is still relevant today. Both men faced as many helps and hindrances in their day as we do now. Vision and its practical application are a matter of determined values harnessed to opportunist strategy and skill. Such impetus and drive can still exist as long as we do not lose faith that ideas and values are fundamental to both personal belief and action:

'Each age is a dream that is dying, and one that is coming to birth.' It was with this quotation from Shelley that Henry Morris opened his address to the British Association at Blackpool in 1936. The dying dream of a state system of schooling geared to eliminate the majority from education before they have come out of their teens is giving way to Morris's dream of a state system where 'We have raised the school leaving age to 90. Where every single being is significated in the economic and social order ... where every local community becomes an educational society, and where education becomes not merely a consequence of good government, but good government a consequence of education' (Rée, 1984, p 144).

Bibliography

Abbs, Peter (1979) *Reclamations*, Heinemann Educational Books.

Angus, Lawrence (1989) ' "New Leadership" and the possibility of education reform' in Smyth, J (ed) *Critical Perspectives on Educational Leadership*, Falmer Press.

Arnold, Matthew (1932) *Culture and Anarchy*, Cambridge University Press.

Bach, Peter and Christensen, Chresten Sloth (1992) 'From despair to optimism: the success story of Danish education', address to RSA, 19 February 1992, *RSA Journal*, vol, CXL, no. 5430.

Barth, Roland S (1990) *Improving Schools from Within*, Jossey Bass.

Bolton, Eric (1992) 'Imaginary gardens with real toads', speech delivered to CLEA, paras 19, 21, 23.

Butcher, John (1990) 'The education and training needs of the 1990s', speech delivered to the RSA, 14 March 1990, *RSA Journal*, vol. CXXXVIII, no. 5409, August 1990, 613-14.

DfE (1991) White Paper *Education and Training for the 21st Century*, HMSO.

DfE (1992) White Paper *Choice and Diversity: A new framework for schools*, HMSO.

Friedman, Milton (1955) 'The role of government in education', in Solo, Robert A (ed), *Economics and the Public Interest*, Rutgers University Press.

Green, Howard (1991), record of meeting with HMIs at DES, 29 July 1991, re: Educational Values Development Programme (EVDP), NEAC.

Greenfield, T B (1986) 'The decline and fall of science in educational administration', *Interchange*, 17, 2, 57-80.

Hayek, F (1978) 'New studies in philosophy', *Politics, Economics and the History of Ideas*, Routledge & Kegan Paul.

Hirschman, Albert O (1970) *Exit, Voice, and Loyalty – Responses to Decline in Firms, Organizations, and States*, Harvard University Press.

Kogan, Maurice (1985) 'Education policy and values' in McNay, I and Ozga, J (eds), *Policy-Making in Education – The Breakdown of Consensus*, Pergamon Press.

MacIntyre, Alasdair (1987) *Education and Values*, the Richard Peters Lectures, Institute of Education, University of London, ed Graham Haydon.

Marquand, David (1988) *The Unprincipled Society*, Fontana.

Morris, Henry (1926/1984) 'Institutionalism and freedom in education', *New Ideals Quarterly*, issued by the Committee of New Ideals in Education, vol. 2, no. 1, March 1926, republished in *The Henry Morris Collection*, Cambridge University Press.

Nietzsche, Friedrich (1965) *Schopenhauer as Educator*, Regnery/Gateway.

Polanyi, Michael (1965) 'On the modern mind', *Encounter*, vol. XXIV, no. 5, 12-19.

Rée, Harry (1984) 'Morris and the future – his prescriptions and our achievements' in Morris, H (1984).

Sallis, Joan (1988) *Schools, Parents and Governors: a new approach to accountability*, Routledge.

Simon, Brian (1985) *Does Education Matter?*, Lawrence and Wishart.

Tawney, R H (1921) *The Acquisitive Society*, G. Bell & Sons.

Taylor, William (1990) *Rediscovering Teacher Education*, the Peterson Lecture, Annual Meeting of the International Baccalaureate's Council of Foundation, Geneva.

Trethowen, David (1985) 'Creating a leadership style' in Blatchford, R (ed) *Managing the Secondary School*, Bell and Hyman.

West, Sylvia (1991) 'Values and the arts' in 'All-In Success', *Journal of the Centre for the Study of Comprehensive Schools*, vol. 3, no. 5, p 26.

White, John (1990) *Education and the Good Life*, London Education Studies, Kogan Page.

White, John (1987), 'The quest for common values', *Education for a Pluralist Society*, Bedford Papers 30, London Institute of Education.

Index